U0135947

2020 潛龍勿用——林章湖書畫展

2020 Hidden Dragon, Do not Act – Lin Chang-hu Ink Painting and Calligraphy Exhibition

展覽期間｜ 2020.2.13（四）– 2020.3.24（二）
地　　點｜中山國家畫廊
開放時間｜上午 9 時 – 下午 6 時
主辦單位｜國立國父紀念館

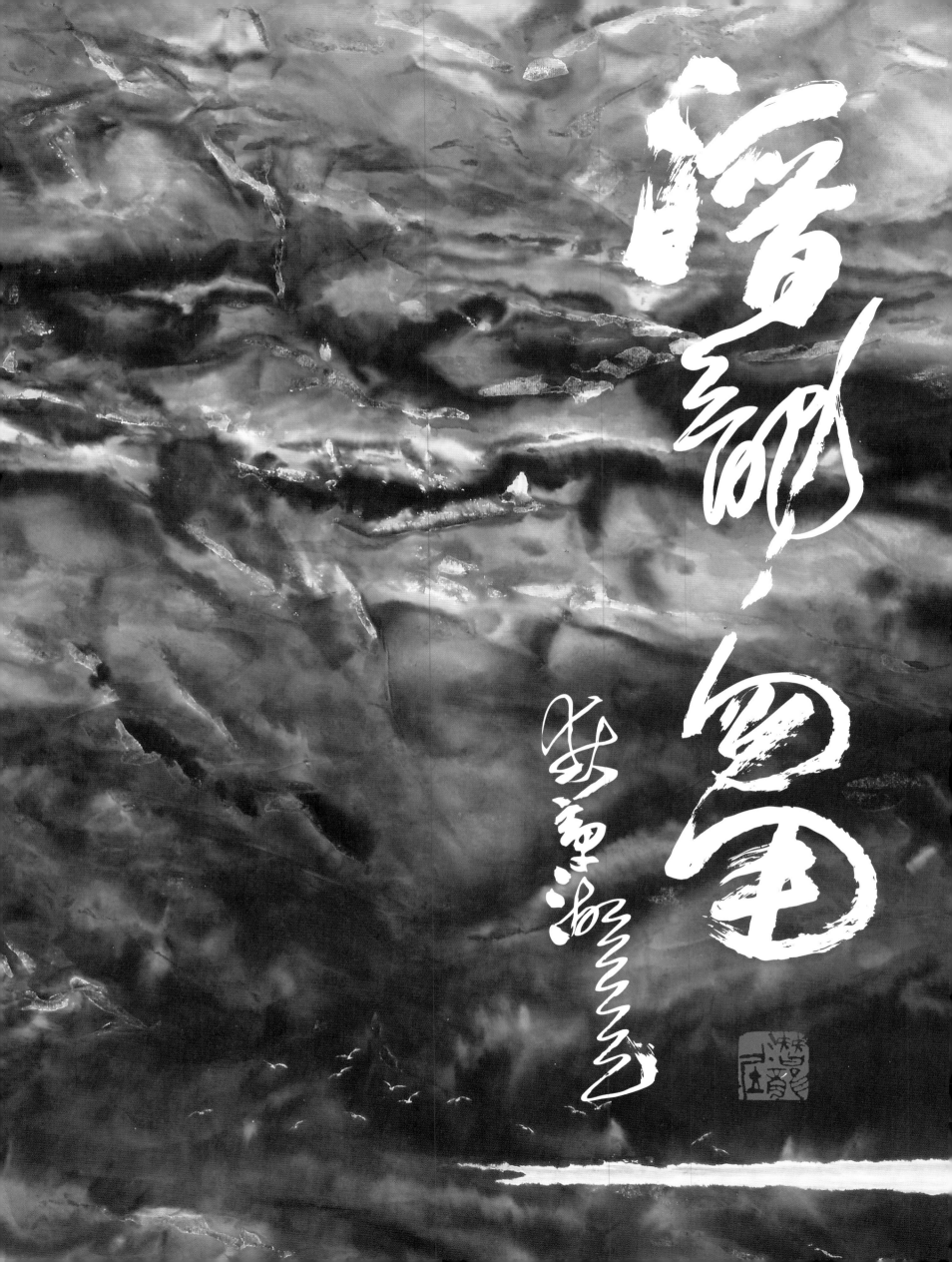

目錄

部長序

　　文化藝術是一個國家的靈魂，透過一件件作品，我們能感受創作技法的奧妙，更能領略創作者的心靈風景與其欣賞世界的視角。書畫藝術家林章湖教授自幼習畫，詩書印畫兼擅，22 歲即獲國家文藝獎肯定，在從事創作之外，林教授更致力投入美術教育，進而持續專研美術研究，精神令人敬佩。

　　林章湖教授的作品致力表現出後現代水墨的豐富性與可能性，在他的作品主題裡，風景、人物、花鳥、走獸皆有，藉由傳統筆墨的熟稔技巧筆法與墨色層次，搭配現代視角的構圖、思想與線條運用，表現了寫景、寫情、寫意的水墨風情。

　　這次國父紀念館以「2020 潛龍勿用—林章湖書畫展」為題，展出林章湖教授水墨、書法、篆刻、詩文及著作共百餘件，完整呈現林教授對水墨創作與研究的經歷。感謝林教授長年投身藝術創作的熱情與精彩作品的提供，誠摯邀請愛好藝術的朋友共同參與展覽。

文化部 部長

Preface by Minister

Culture and art are the soul of a country. Through the artworks, we can feel the profoundness of the creative skills and understand the creators' landscape in mind and their angles to appreciate the world. The calligraphy and painting artist, Prof. Lin Chang-hu, has learned painting since childhood and excelled in poetry, calligraphy, seal carving, and painting. He won National Cultural and Arts Award when he was only twenty-two. Besides engaging in creation, Prof. Lin is also dedicated to art education and further art studies. His spirit is admirable.

Prof. Lin Chang-hu have spared no effort to express the richness and possibility of postmodern ink painting in his works. The topics of his works include landscape, figures, flowers and birds, and animals. The skillful techniques and ink levels of traditional ink painting are accompanied by the composition, thinking, and line application from the modern angle to express the charm of the scenery, feeling, and image in ink painting.

This time, in the exhibition titled "2020 Hidden Dragon, Do not Act – Lin Chang-hu Ink Painting and Calligraphy Exhibition," National Dr. Sun Yat-sen Memorial Hall exhibits more than one hundred works of Prof. Lin Chang-hu, including ink painting, calligraphy, seal carving, poetry, and publications to completely present Prof. Lin's experience in ink art creation and research. We are grateful to Prof. Lin for dedicating himself to art creation with passion and for offering the great works. We sincerely invite the art lovers to visit the exhibition together.

Minister of Culture Cheng Li-chiun

館長序

　　林章湖教授 1955 年出生於新北市。

　　1977 年，年方弱冠即獲國家文藝獎，1987 年獲教育部文藝創作獎、1989 年獲第一屆大陸吳作人國際青年美術獎、2004 年獲中華民國畫學會金爵獎，可說是天才型藝術家。曾於國內外應邀參加過無數展覽，地點遍及臺灣、都柏林、東京、漢城、新加坡、紐約、華盛頓、舊金山、約堡、坎培拉、西貢、開封、 北京、上海、廣州、南京、杭州等。作品獲國立臺灣美術館、臺北市立美術館、高雄市立美術館、國立臺灣師範大學及臺灣創價學會等美術館典藏。

　　林章湖教授的繪畫天份於少年時期即受到注目及肯定，其詩書畫印兼具，可謂全方位藝術家。但更讓人敬佩的是 2010 年自台北藝術大學退休後，前往中國中央美院攻讀博士學程，最後以《「後現代」與台灣當代水墨》論文取得博士頭銜，實踐其「以藝術作為學術之體、學術作為藝術之用」之理念。

　　林教授創作融合書法、繪畫與篆刻，強調內在精神及外在表象的實踐，展現具文人書卷底蘊的後現代式水墨，本次展出林教授水墨、書法、篆刻、詩文及著作百餘件，件件精品，完整呈現其對水墨創作與研究的經歷，林教授在藝術創作及理論研究的表現有目共睹。

　　本館長年致力推廣文化藝術及生活美學，持續邀請藝術界具重要貢獻的藝術家於本館中山國家畫廊展出。感謝林教授提供精選創作展出。誠摯邀請愛好藝術的朋友，共同分享。

國立國父紀念館 館長

Preface by Director-General

Prof. Lin Chang-hu was born in New Taipei City in 1955. In 1977, he won Na-tional Cultural and Arts Award in his twenties. He was given Creative Literature and Arts Awards of Ministry of Education in 1987, the first Wu Zuoren International Art Award in 1989, and the gold award of The Art Society of China in 2004. He can be regarded as an artist with genius. He held numerous exhibitions at home and abroad, including Taiwan, Dublin, Tokyo, Seoul, Singapore, New York, Washington, San Francisco, Johannesburg, Canberra, Saigon, Kaifeng, Beijing, Shanghai, Guangzhou, Nanjing, and Hangzhou. His works are collected in National Taiwan Museum of Fine Arts, Taipei Fine Arts Museum, Kaohsiung Museum of Fine Arts, National Taiwan Normal University, and Taiwan Soka Association.

Prof. Lin Chang-hu's painting talent has stood out and been acclaimed since boyhood. Excelling in poetry, calligraphy, painting, and seal carving, he can be seen as a versatile artist. It is admirable that he went to study in the PhD program in Cen-tral Academy of Fine Arts and received the doctorate with the dissertation, 'Post-modernism' and the Contemporary Ink Painting in Taiwan, putting into practice the idea of "Art serves as the body of academic studies, and academic studies can be ap-plied to art."

Prof. Lin's creation integrates calligraphy, painting, and seal carving, empha-sizing the practice of inner spirit and outer appearance and showing the postmodern ink painting with the literati's cultural profoundness. This time we exhibit more than one hundred works of Prof. Lin's ink painting, calligraphy, seal carving, poetry, and publications. All of them are the exquisite works completely presenting his experi-ence in ink creation and research. Prof. Lin's achievement in art creation and theo-retical research are well known. Our hall has been devoted to promoting cultural art and life aesthetics for long and continued to invite the artists with the important con-tribution in the art circle to hold exhibitions at Chungshan National Gallery of our hall. We are grateful to Prof. Lin for providing his selected creations for the exhibi-tion. We sincerely invite art lovers to join and share with us.

Director-General of National Dr. Sun Yat-sen Memorial Hall

Liang Yung-fei

水墨畫新世紀的美學詮釋者與創作者

黃光男｜國立臺灣藝術大學前校長

　　藝術工作者在習藝歷程，必得才能、理趣與意氣，亦即在時空進行中洞悉社會發展，歷史陳述與文化進程，得在多方攝取中化為創作的力量。四十多年前，曾在林章湖畢業展觀賞他以白鷺佇停竹林之花鳥大作，頓時被此畫一股新鮮有機筆墨震住。在當時水墨界一股腦以文人畫形式作為美質標示時，見這幅畫之「生意」與「大氣」，方知師大藝術教育傳授「寫生」論之成效。令人感動者，林章湖仍然在文質彬彬之中，力求「畫者，須息心靜氣、再三思索」理念，數十年勤奮不懈，然後含毫伸紙、先造形後造境，乃至神致雋趣，藝境大氣磅礡。

文化積澱與新生

　　文人畫質中，以「學問、思想、品德與才華」作為書畫家必修內質，林章湖四項均在潛移默化進行永續「苟日新、又日新」工程，惟才華泰半先天即在經師道傳授而成。我較為好奇者他進入師大名師教導前，是否有啟蒙老師或家學淵源之影響，即得才華四溢。至少感人詞句與定標於畫作題款，即顯現不同於同儕道友，除在畫面表達他另有主張的豐盛。再三忖度，他對傳統文明即為經驗之回溯，不論是「六法」、「六要」或一脈相承之文化體中之「…逸筆草草」或無法為法之美學詮釋，耳聽八方、眼看四方，務求中華文化體現在自己畫作上。即所謂「溫故知新」之清朗與前行。

　　文化是知識、思想、情感之經驗，也是「某特定社會的成員共享並相互傳遞知識、態度、習慣性行為模式等之總和」。如此而言，文化的社會性、歷史性與生活模式，正引導藝術家創作之價值體察，且是創作者經驗取得的美學養份。

　　林章湖遵從名師提示，又得自我修為，傳統文化數千年的積澱，何人可知可感而達其共知共感，林章湖是其中佼佼者。藝壇更敬佩他在文化傳承過程中存菁棄蕪，即時代環境以「現象學」之精神，進行新舊之間之認知與選擇。所以他的論點，也採取後現代美學，後文人畫與新文人畫，以及將現代國際藝壇常使用之語彙來解釋傳統意涵，在這歷程中他主張水墨畫如建築界所發動「後現代主義」，將優質且具美學要素之形質予保留與填充，亦即筆墨基礎之哲學思考，多層美學意涵彙集成河，順暢注入藝術創作之核心，或激流浪花力道強勁，或可映現時空倒影。它即是藝術表現之本體，亦得現實即現代性之視覺對象。這項經驗來自他不斷研究與實踐，亦為他在水墨畫新境界的開始，包括物象新視野與技法應用與嘗試，當然所有技法均為畫境表現之形式，卻是新造境之必要功夫，即如古人說是骨法用筆是氣韻生動的基礎。

〈旭日翔鷗〉圖版 p.62

　　這是水墨畫新視界的開端，加上他在水墨美學上之認知，更導入美感創作的基礎，所以活在「墨分五色」，淡者分層，畫境在有無之中見真章。好比他在〈旭日翔鷗〉畫作中，墨之層次濃淡、乾濕、黑白分層，正是濃者為陰，淡者為陽外，濃墨要火候，有重筆才得體；而淡者要清神，方得筆墨之趣，即便以西畫論述亦然也，此項新生意境林章湖有不言之妙。

水墨畫現場

水墨畫現場對於林章湖而言，是項「盈天地之間者，萬物皆含毫運思」之工作。換言之，古今物象皆然，現象各異，觀時序變遷，現象易境，是為繪畫藝術美之支架，其中得有心靈流動滋潤於景物者，被選擇之物象或時令物體，均在時人習慣或寄望之圖記，甚至如科技中「虛擬實境」之理念，甚至為咫尺千里，一物萬象之濃興與寄情。唐人詩有「嫩綠枝頭紅一點，動人春色不須多」，物與象，即心與美，若得靈犀則古月為今月，今月亦明月之常性與常理。

林章湖在水墨畫藝術創作過程中審視當下，社會意識之流動，並深切了解西方藝術學對水墨畫創作之衝擊，從畫作看得出他極力尋求東方美學系統之詮釋，也以國際現實作為一系列深入探求「境界」。境即為物象與意象之間的布局，包括情思的反芻，或是視覺經驗陳述，其美學感知是物我之間靈動力量。在此有二項要求，一則社會之參予，應用人性之普遍性，以己之能量將藝術創作提升精神溫度，感染社會在此活動（創作）中得到感情解放，二是在作品中加入與之相契共識人群中得以融和。

關於此項目標，在結合藝術美與觀眾遇合情愫，若與現實性而言，畫面當蘊含創作者精神力量，通過嶄新（創作力）之形式再起意象之寄情，此情境有新舊交織，互為依賴理念，並為需求與消融之經濟情節，亦藝術家與觀眾之間，有一道明亮且通往美感亮光，焦聚在畫面之形質，林章湖明確創作經驗在水墨畫內容與形式用心，基於上述情境互補理論得到創作動能，舒解中國繪畫近世紀以來「以西潤中」或「神遊象外」之論斷，既得形式之純粹，亦得意境之圓融。

社會性源於集體意識凝聚，以縱向時間理解歷史繪畫經驗，得有文化基因以為創作力量；橫向則在國際與環境呈現多元藝術表現時，該給予認識與自我體驗為行動，正如佛說法，縱口極談，拈往因果，繪畫者胸中實有，筆墨可親則是。林章湖藝術美之現場古往今來，美感鮮活矣！

遊藝自在

近來得有機會拜讀林章湖作品，又得其文質理氣充實畫面，甚為佩服，除已見其水墨畫清新脫俗，氣象盈滿外，更欣見他在書法與詩詞之造詣，不覺令人想起詩（詞）、書、畫同源之說，亦覺其浸涉文學之勤，乃為藝壇傑出之創作者，以及東方藝術之可貴，在於神、逸、巧、能之中「還元」之運行，亦即為中國藝術精神在儒、道、釋之結合，尤其道可道，非常道…之運作。與人格即畫格之寄興，得有藝術本質之用心，非當求其皮毛而已。

再說林章湖修養心性之餘，不失其常德與常道，親和常德於前，堅持常理於後，使之藝術造境中出現盤礴睥睨，磊磊落落之勢，亦為人格之尊也。其說亦可審賞其書法藝術之追索，在筆墨合一之中，從整齊悅目開始，實者悟書法者「巧涉丹青，工虧翰墨」即同於圖畫之喻。此理即中國藝術表現中書畫同源之論，或說他於書法之表現，有如繪畫之創作，字形即為結構，間架即為圖地，而能活其造形者，乃基於點、線、面與墨色之調配，成為活性有機之結合圖像，尤其應用中文字體之肇造，以六書之象形、形聲、會意、指事、假借、轉注體例，重現中國書法之美。象形固然有圖可尋，形聲則完型節奏之性，會意亦在加強符號寄情之圖記，餘此類推。林章湖書藝大致基於這項因素，造就他如「龍跳天門，虎臥鳳闕」藝術美。欣賞他的書法，即是與繪畫共體之結構，而活性運筆揮墨不僅外在技法，也是生機性再造筆墨，沁人心弦。

造形美即是裝飾美，也是抽象美，圖面有畫、有書、尚得有文字。文字者文人之情思也，近年水墨壇甚少提倡：「有文人之味道」詩詞吟唱於畫面中，造成水墨畫流於形式視覺之展現，未能在可知可感可歌之內容上增溫，類為有形無神之類。林章湖明白且視為改進之路並審視水墨畫之再生，對於新文人畫，或後文人畫多所感應，於是在傳統古文學上力求精進與創意，不論有韻之古詩絕律兩便，或散文押韻歌詠畫面外之情狀，正所謂「詩傳畫外意」，此乃水墨畫之綜合藝術之論，西方學者蘇立文早已說到「現代中國水墨畫非僅圖象，而是意象、抽象共體之綜合藝術」，那麼林章湖勤奮於文學的創作與開發，不論書法與詩詞加入畫面上，所達到之水墨畫境界，豈有不被推崇之理。

美學詮釋者與創作者

同為追求水墨畫新世紀的美學詮釋者與創作者，對於林章湖水墨境的造境，多少有幾分的共感，且在作品中林章湖所表現的藝術美，以及水墨畫時代性風格的新生體，均可再探索中得到深切的理解，尤其前述所說的傳統與現代的關係，取決於他自身的才華與學養。其所處的時空與創作原素的攝取，具備了幾項特質：自然體、社會體與藝術體的融合與突破，正如社會學家韋伯 (M. E.Weber) 曾以自然觀察與理解分辨來解釋傳統與現代，經驗與知識的成長或依恃。

具體地說，林章湖在承受傳統的美學觀與創作時有二個原素在他的筆墨技法上出現。亦即水墨畫的寫生論，即是觀察自然生態所累績的「經驗」，是自身對物象的敏感度，或稱之為見人所未見，知人所不知，卻又是不得不知的道理，這項理路有人也持之為才華的展現，此其一；其次是知識來自前人的「經驗」，是傾向學習的過程，包含創作規律、內容與技法，不論是自身的體驗或是傳統所規範的形質，林章湖的學習反射在「有為者亦若是」的心性，將原有的文化體保留了精華形體，以繽紛燦爛之形質，重塑繪畫藝術的主體性。

林章湖當然清楚主體性與客體性的表現，源於身心交織的結果。所謂主體性是所要表現的對象是他者還是我者，是模仿自然還是創造自然？是真實的自我，還是社會通性的外溢。在此應該涉及了現實與想像，理性與感性的攝取。若藝術工作的創作過程有二個現象可以簡述為跟隨者與引導者，那麼這二項的共同造境該是藝術發展的重要鑰匙。

詮釋者是學習、接納與其審美的過程，林章湖自小就在文化體系上了解文化即是知識累積所形式的創作興味，以及追求美感的審美認知，包括他時時不忘水墨畫形態的表現，分享他所體悟到的文化精華，這項過程包括水墨畫中的美學符號，是知識情感與理想的結合，或筆墨、或色調、或結構不一而足，既有文人的寄興，亦得暗喻、明喻或傳誦、表彰的文詞，不全是詩詞的定向，也是畫外畫的變易，知者亦深，悟者更明的畫境。

創作者對林章湖來說，更具現代性的張力，看似平常題材，卻是引領視覺經驗的新生，因為經驗來自想像的造景，以自我的才能，即所謂的天才來啟發學習的興味，在作品上暢述「三才」的創作，而後達到藝術創作的新型態。前二者是交互影響的，但二者之間鮮活在現象學所謂的整體，則非有超越現象的環境能力不可，林章湖的學習與創作，不謹是二者兼具更有人為（荀子）與自然（老子）藝術的整體領悟，並且明確而細心在自個環境發揮二者交融的現場。

藝術家藉將整體資源運用，並全面吸收人為與自然特性於其作品之材料中，必然會產生一種新的藝術創作，亦即在造境的過程中，自我涵養是新藝術與新境界的光譜。自我涵養是主客體的整體運作，也是美學所標示的哲理與符碼應用，好比改善視覺習慣，賦予符號特微，表彰美感價值等是否成為創作的必要條件，雖然無肯定它的完善價值，但如林章湖的悉心於藝術主體寄於現象經驗時，藝術美的湧現，絕對是他自身或自我情感的外溢，畫面充滿生命的溫度，此一現象正如美學家柯林伍德（R.G. Collingwood）所說：「我們在客體所見的美，原是自我們自己的功能，而非歸功於客體中的任何真實力量」，這項說法就如莊子所說：「子非我，豈知我不知魚之樂」的思索。

　　基於「美是透過想像客體之全部經驗的情感特色」，我們發覺林章湖創作的動力，在於人性與文化認同的整體，也在於社會意識所匯集的情知，並且有了相當審美藝術的激發力量，尤其看到他近作〈池中魚〉的情境，古早生活境界躍然畫面。生活包含了人生觀、宇宙觀的遇合。人籟、地籟、天籟附著於筆墨流動上，開啟了「大塊噫氣，其名曰風」的情態，與人氣接壤，與天地萬物共感的生態，既得物象之始，又明示意象之發，此乃為藝術美之實相，亦是林章湖幾十年來，參禪似的明燈。所謂默契神會畫面表現的「景、情、境」，在於物象、意象與立象之結合，它明確闡明繪畫藝術在現象與實相之間的轉換，也說明了創作者，應用情智前的技法修為，豈只是筆墨靈巧或記憶猶新的場域！

　　林章湖創作論藝是心手合一，情理並蓄，正是「吾寫此紙時，心入春江水，江花隨我開，江水隨我起」（石濤）的境界。詩書畫三絕之於林章湖藝術表現與理想，件件作品均在閃爍光芒。不論寫生剪裁、美感造境或意象營造，在「得之天機，生於靈府」之餘，他出入在藝術史長流裡，亦得有文化傳承上中流砥柱。滔滔之聲，是他勤奮節奏；閒閒之智是他的道行。他掌握時代，睥睨環境，發揮才華與能量，是位令人感動的藝術家。

〈池中魚〉圖版 p.81

The Aesthetic Interpreter and Creator of New Century Ink Painting

Huang Kuang-nan | Former President of National Taiwan University of Arts

In the process of art learning, an art worker has to acquire the talent, appeal, and spirit. That is, he has to have insight into social development, historical narration, and cultural progression to gain the creative power from a variety of absorption.

Forty years ago, I went to appreciate Lin Chang-hu's flower and bird painting featuring egrets resting in the bamboo forest at the graduation exhibition and was shocked by the fresh and organic ink brushstrokes in the painting. At that time, when the ink painting world went all out to regard literati painting as the aesthetic standard, I found the effects of NTNU's focus on "sketching" in art education when finding "life" and "grandeur" in the painting. What's more touching is that Lin Chang-hu, with a gentle nature, sticks to the concept that "a painter has to rest his mind, keep calm, and think again" and keeps working diligently for decades. Conceive the idea, spread the paper, create the style and atmosphere, and then the spirit and charm. All these lead to the grand and majestic art level.

Cultural Accumulation and New Life

In the quality of literati painting, "knowledge, thinking, character, and talent" are the required cultivation for a calligrapher or a painter. Lin Chang-hu has been sustainably and naturally developing the four elements day by day. A man's talents tend to be inborn and then developed with the teachers' teaching. I am more curious whether his great talent comes from the inspiration of an abecedarian or family influence before receiving the instruction of the famous teachers in NTNU.

At least, the touching phrases and markings on the painting inscription are shown in a different way from other peer painters. The image displays his unique view of richness. To take a closer look, his traditional civilization is to recall the past experiences. Be it "Six Rules," "Six Principles," "···carefree brushstrokes" in the cultural context of the same lineage, or the aesthetic interpretation in a form without a form, by listening to all directions and seeing all sides, he spares no effort to manifest the Chinese culture in his paintings. In other words, it is the so-called clarity and moving forward by "reviewing what has been learned and learning something new."

Culture is the experience of knowledge, thinking, and feeling, and also "the sum total of the knowledge, attitudes, and habitual behavior patterns shared and transmitted by the members of a society." Accordingly, the sociality, historic significance, and lifestyle of the culture are the guidance to artists' value observation in creation and the aesthetic nutrients acquired with the creators' experience.

Besides following the famous teachers' suggestions, Lin Chang-hu also cultivates himself through the accumulation of the traditional culture for thousands of years. Few people could achieve his level of perception and feeling, for he is the best of the best. The art world also admires him for discarding the weeds and retaining the flowers in the process of cultural heritage. With the spirit of "phenomenology," the era and the environment also make recognitions and choice between the new and the old.

Therefore, his argument also adopts postmodernist aestheticism, post-literati painting, and new literati painting and interprets the traditional meaning with the lexicons commonly used in the modern international art world. In the process, he contends that ink painting, like "postmodernism" proposed by the architecture field, retains and fills the quality character with the aesthetic elements. In other words, the philosophical thinking of the basic brushstrokes and the multi-layered aesthetic meaning are combined and infused smoothly into the core of art creation, creating the powerful torrential spray or reflecting the image of time and space. It is the body of art expression and the visual object of reality and modernity.

The experience comes from his continuous research and practice, the start point of his new level in ink painting, including the new horizon of the image and the application and attempt of techniques. Indeed, all techniques are the forms of painting expression as well as the required skills to explore the new territory. As the ancients said, they are the basis for brushstrokes and vividness.

This is the beginning of the new horizon of ink painting. Besides, his perception of ink aestheticism is introduced to the basis of the aesthetic creation. As "ink is divided into five shades," the painting expression is revealed in the different layers. For example, in his painting "Flying Seagull at Sunrise," the ink layers lie between strong and light, dry or wet, black and white. That is, the strong shade is Yin; the light shade is Yang. The strong ink has to go with heavy strokes to make the style consistent. The light ink has to go with clarity to display the fun of ink. This is also true with western painting. Lin Chang-hu has the self-evident talent for the new expression.

On the Scene of Ink Painting

For Lin Chang-hu, ink painting is the work that "brushes everything in heaven and earth with the conception." In other words, in both ancient and modern times, from the different phenomena, the changes of time can be observed. The various phenomena serve as the framework of beauty in the art of painting. As an artist's mental flow nourishes the objects, the chosen object or seasonal target is transformed into the image through the creator's habit or expectation. It's even like the concept of "virtual reality" in technology and even making the objects thousand miles away close at hand. One object is endowed with the charm and passion of everything in the world. In one Tang poem, "Above the tender green on the branch, one dot of red/To move men, spring's colors need not be abundant." As the object is to the image, mind is to beauty. With the inspiration, it is common and normal that the ancient moon can represent the present moon, and the present moon will embody the future moon.

In the process of art creation of ink painting, Lin Chang-hu examines the flow of social consciousness at present and deeply understands the impact of western art thinking on the creation of ink painting. From his paintings, we can find his endeavor to seek the interpretation of the oriental aesthetic system and make a series of deep explorations of the "realm" through international reality. The realm is the layout between the object and the image, including the reflection on feelings or the narration of visual experiences. The aesthetic perception is the spiritual power between the object and the subject. There are two requirements here. One is social participation. Through the universality of humanity, the personal power will increase the spiritual temperature with the art works and influence the society which will experience the emotional liberation in this activity (creative work). Second is to add the congeniality and consensus to the works and integrate into the public.

Regarding this goal to combine the beauty of art and the congeniality of the viewers, in terms of reality, the image picture should be endowed with the creator's spiritual power and create the sensitivities in the image in a brand new (creative) form. The situation is interwoven with the old and the new, which depend on each other. It is like an economic plot between need and disappearance. That is, between an artist and his viewers, there is a bright ray leading to a sense of beauty focused on the character of the picture. Lin Chang-hu's clear creative experience is devoted to the content and form of ink painting. He gains his creative energy based on the theory of complementary situations mentioned above and gets rid of the arguments about "borrowing the western spirit in the Chinese works" or "wandering out of the image" of the Chinese painting in the recent centuries, achieving both the purity of the form and the integrity of the realm.

Sociality originates from the cohesion of collected consciousness. Vertically, the historical painting experience is understood in terms of the different periods of time. The cultural genes are taken as the creative power. Horizontally, when the diverse art performances are presented to the world and the environment, there should be the action for personal knowledge and experience. As Buddha expounds the dharma, the ultimate truth is shared in the random talks connecting to the cause and effect. The painter's intrinsic talents can be accessed through brushes and ink. The artistic beauty in Lin Chang-hu's works is vivid throughout the ages!

Wandering Freely in the World of Art

Recently, I have the chance to read Lin Chang-hu's works and admire very much that his literary talent and momentum enriches the image even more. Besides his fresh and refined ink painting full of expressions, I am more amazed by his cultivation in calligraphy and poetry, which reminds me of the theory that poetry, calligraphy, and painting share the same origin. I have felt his diligent indulgence in literature and considered him an outstanding creator in the art world. The valuable part of the oriental art lies in the operation of "returning" in spirit, ease, ingenuity, and capability. In other words, it is the combination of the Chinese art spirit with Confucianism, Taoism, and Buddhism, especially in the operation of "The way that can be told is not the usual way." With the connotation that personality is reflected on painting styles, the devotion to the essence of art is never skin deep.

Furthermore, besides cultivating himself, Lin Chang-hu also follows the universal morality and general ethics. By familiarizing himself with the universal morality and insisting on the general ethics, he creates the magnificent grandeur in his art style and the strength of uprightness in his personality. In his exploration of calligraphy art, the unification of the brush and ink starts from tidiness and beauty. The realization of calligraphy is more like the expression of painting than the art of brush and ink. This is the theory in the Chinese art expression that calligraphy and painting share the same origin. In other words, his calligraphy is like the creation of painting. As the script is to the structure, the frame is to the composition. The gist of the style comes from the arrangement of points, lines, planes, and ink colors, which are all combined into an organic image with life. Moreover, the application of the six ways of composing Chinese characters, pictographs(Xiang Xing), phono-semantic compounds(Xing Sheng), compound ideographs(Hui Yi), Simple ideograms(Zhi Shi), rebus or phonetic loan characters(Jia Jie), and derivative cognates(Zhuan Zhu) represent the beauty of Chinese calligraphy. Xiang Xing is to follow the image, Xing Sheng is to complete the rhythm, Hui Yi is to strengthen the symbolic mark, and so on. Lin Chang-hu's calligraphy art is generally based on this factor, which contributes to the beauty of his art with a spirit of "a dragon leaping to the heavenly gate and a tiger crouching in the royal court." The appreciation of his calligraphy has to be focused on the unification with painting. The lively use of brushstrokes and ink does not only show the external technique but also create the vitality striking a chord with the viewers.

The beauty of style is the beauty of decoration as well as the beauty of abstraction. In the picture, there are painting, calligraphy, and words. The words are the literati's thinking. In recent years, in the ink painting circle there has been little promotion of the poetic chanting with "the literati's taste" in the image, which makes ink painting tend to be the visual performance of formality without the temperature in the contents for perception, feeling, and praise. Most of the works are with the appearance but without the spirit. Lin Chang-hu realizes the phenomenon and makes the improvements by examining the new path for ink painting. He shares the same thought with new literati painting or post-literati painting; therefore, he pursues progress and creativity in traditional classical literature whether in terms of the quatrains and octonaries with rhymes or the rhymed prose celebrating the situations out of the image. This is the so-called "poetry expressing the meaning behind the picture," the comprehensive art theory of ink painting. As the western scholar Michael Sullivan said, modern Chinese ink painting is not only the image but also the art combination of imagery and abstraction. Judging from this, Lin Chang-hu's hard work in the literary creation and development by adding calligraphy and poetry to the image and the ink painting level he's achieved have all the reason to be acclaimed.

Aesthetic Interpreter and Creator

As an aesthetic interpreter and creator of new century ink painting, I share some same feelings with Lin Chang-hu's conception of ink painting and have a deep understanding in exploring the artistic beauty expressed in his works and the new products of the ink painting style in the era, especially the relationship between tradition and modernity mentioned above depending on his personal talents and cultivation. The absorption of the creative elements in his time and space has several characteristics: the integration and breakthrough of nature, society, and art. Similarly, the sociologist M. E. Weber used to explain the growth and reliance on experience and knowledge in the traditional and modern world through the natural observation and understanding

In general, inheriting from the traditional aesthetic concept and creation, Lin Chang-hu has two elements in his ink painting techniques. That is, the sketching theory of ink painting is the "experience" accumulated with the observation of natural ecology. It is the personal sensitivity to objects, or the way to see what others can't see, know what others don't know, and have no choice but to know it. On the one hand, this can also be regarded as the display of the talent. On the other hand, knowledge comes from the predecessors' "experience." It tends to be a process of learning, including the creative patterns, contents, and techniques. Whether it is the personal experience or the quality regulated by tradition, Lin Chang-hu's learning reflects the mind that "one can always achieve something as long as he works hard and models after the sages." He retains the quintessence of the original culture and reshapes the subjectivity of the art of painting with the splendid quality.

Lin Chang-chu knows clearly that the performance of subjectivity and objectivity originates from the mingling result of body and mind. Is the object which is expressed by the so-called subjectivity the other or the self? Does it imitate nature or create nature? Is it the true self or the overflow of the social common nature? This should be connected to the absorption of reality and imagination, sense and sensibility. If there are two phenomena in the creative process of the artwork which can be concluded as the follower and the leader, the mental level shared by the two should be the important key to the development of art.

An interpreter goes through the process of learning, acceptance, and artistic conception. Since childhood, in the cultural system, Lin Chang-hu has understood that culture is the creative interest formed with the knowledge accumulation and the aesthetic cognition in pursuit of aestheticism. He often keeps in mind the expression of the ink painting style and shares the cultural essence in his realization. The process includes the aesthetic symbols in ink painting, which are the combination of knowledge, feeling, ideal, ink, color tones, structure, and all the other perspectives. With the literati's sentiment, metaphor, simile, or the words of reciting and of praise, they are not necessarily the poetic direction but the varieties of the painting outside of painting, achieving the painting level that the informed ones will know things better and the enlightened ones will see things more clearly.

For Lin Chang-hu, a creator has the modern tension. The seemingly ordinary topics can lead to the new life of visual experience because experience comes from the imaginary scene making. The personal talent, the so-called genius, will inspire the interest in learning. In works, he fluently expresses the creation of "three talents" and later achieves the new style of the artistic creation. The former two have the mutual effect on each other. However, if the two are to coexist in the so-called totality in phenomenology, there have to be the environmental capacity to surpass the phenomenon. Lin Chang-hu's learning and creation are equipped not only with both but also with the overall realization of the artificial (Xunzi) and natural (Laozi) art and clearly and carefully exerts the mixture of both in the environment they belong to.

By applying the overall resources and completing absorbing the artificial and natural characteristics in the materials of the works, an artist will create a new form of art creation. In other words, in the process of creating the atmosphere, self cultivation is the spectrum of new art and new level. Self cultivation is the overall operation of subjectivity and objectivity as well as the philosophical and symbolic application marked in aesthetics. For example, whether improving the visual habits, endowing the symbolic characteristics, or manifesting the aesthetic value can become the requirements of creation. Though the complete value is not affirmed, Lin Chang-hu's careful devotion of the phenomenon and experience to the art objects and the emergence of the artistic beauty are absolutely the overflow of the self or personal feelings, filling the picture with the temperature of life. The phenomenon is just like what R.G. Collingwood said: The beauty we perceive in the object comes from our own function instead of being attributed to any real power in the object. The argument is similar to Zhuangzi's thinking: You are not me. How could you know that I don't understand how happy the fish are?

Based on the idea that beauty is the emotional characteristic with the imagination of all experience of the object, we will find that Lin Chang-hu's creative power lies in the totality recognized by humanity and culture and the affection collected with social consciousness. He also has the inspiration of the aesthetic art, especially in his recent work "Fish in the Pond," where the life atmosphere of old times comes to life in the picture. Life is the encounter of the philosophy of life and the view of universe. The sounds of humanity, earth, and heaven are attached to the flow of ink, creating the condition that "the land's breath is called wind." With the connection to humanity, the shared feeling with everything on earth, the start of natural phenomenon, and the indication of the image prosperity, the real practice of the artistic beauty is Lin Chang-hu's beacon in meditation for decades. The "scene, feeling, and atmosphere" expressed in the picture of tacit understanding consist in the combination of object, imagery, and image establishment. It clearly interprets the transformation of the painting art between phenomenon and reality and also explains the creators' learning of techniques before the emotional and intellectual application. It is never a field of only dexterous skills or fresh memories!

The creative art of Lin Chang-hu is the unification of body and mind and the focus on both feeling and reason, achieving the same level with Shi Tao's poem: "When I write on this paper, my heart is flowing with the water of the river of spring. The flowers by the river blossom with me. The water in the river rises with me. (Shi Tao)" The ideal artistic expression of poetry, calligraphy, and painting in Lin Chang-hu's works shines gloriously. In sketching cutting, aesthetic atmosphere, or imagery creation, with born gifts and talents, he plays the essential role of cultural heritage in the long history of art. He works diligently without stop and attains wisdom composedly. He takes hold of the era, overlooks the environment, and exerts his talent and energy. He is an artist touching people's heart.

章法自在，湖光悠遊：林章湖博士的書畫創思

廖新田 | 國立歷史博物館館長

「自在理想」的創作歷程

林章湖教授，少年時期便顯示出獨樹一幟的繪畫天份，從其臨摹傳統水墨作品判讀，栩栩如生，墨色、構圖、甚至是韻味都頗有架式，讓人驚訝，不免聯想：此人天生就是要吃這行飯，走這條路。

1988 年，林章湖

所謂「三分天注定，七分靠打拼」，他盡情展現才華，孜孜矻矻、力求精進。大三時期，他便獲得第 26 屆師大美術系展 (1976 年) 國畫類第三名 (第一名從缺)；隔年，更上層樓，獲得系展首獎的「教育部長獎」，花鳥作品得到高度讚賞，評論「以成熟的技巧把 [白鷺鷥] 給畫活了。」[1] 林玉山看到這張作品大加讚賞，認為「林同學」將來很快會成才。所言甚是，十數隻散聚的鷺鳥各展其姿，構成一幅生動有機的畫面，在他後來各式主題上也展現這種傑出的構圖經營能力，真的讓畫面活了起來。同時，他的書法作品也拿到第二名，鋪陳出未來將是書畫雙秀的優勢。再傳捷報，當年的畢業美展以《白鷺》拿到首獎，書法第二名，篆刻第三名，後者也埋下他往後精於治印的伏筆。這次，他展現更高超的描寫能力，將為數更多的鷺鳥集聚，各具姿態，栩栩如生，彷彿還可以聽到參差嘈雜鳴聲，融入於密林中。畢業後，因成績優異，被學校薦送 1977 年第五屆「國家文藝獎」大專美術獎項。

《白鷺圖》師大畢業美展第一名

從事教職之際，他積極參與各式大小展覽，相當專注與投入，也藉這些機會鍛鍊自己。72 年度他獲得教育部文藝創作獎獲得第二名，75 年度更獲得第一名。1988 年 10 月，林章湖在臺北市立美術館舉行首次個展。當時報導他的創作觀是「美感經驗的超樣式化和內容形式關係的有機體結構」[2]，以及「理想性」和「表現性」追尋美感高度 [3]，頗異於一般水墨的傳統式評語 (如語詞及引用都是過去規矩制式的畫論觀點)。值得注意的是，不囿於傳統而勇敢創新，則是他和新一代水墨家的共識。

1989 年，北京中國美術館開幕的第七屆全國美展邀請林章湖、林昌德、蕭進發、陳宏勉、程代勒、張克齊等人前往觀摩，林章湖竟「意外」以《瀧之溯魚》獲得「吳作人國際美術基金會青年獎」，獎金 3000 人民幣，但是他把獎金回捐，以感謝他們的肯定。同獲殊榮的是遼寧魯迅美術學院講師韋爾申 (現任魯迅美術學院院長)。吳作人給這位年輕新秀的題詞是「華香兩岸」，顯示他的創作獲得兩岸的共鳴。這個殊榮，恐怕到目前為止都是極為獨特的紀錄。

吳作人題詞「華香兩岸」

除自己選送文藝創作獎之外，林章湖從不參與美術競賽，都是被動頒贈，不主動爭取。以他年少才華盡展之態，若有企圖，當會頗有斬獲。他認為創作是純粹的追求，比賽拿獎

1　陳以誠，1977，〈「心有千千結」師大美展觀後〉，《雄獅美術》73 期。按：應該是夜鷺。

2　《聯合報》，1988/10/9，5 版。根據該年出版的《林章湖畫選》，自序中對「超樣式化」的解釋是：運用新技法表達感受，「有機體結構」強調動態氣勢的構圖。

3　李玉玲，1988/10/11，〈林章湖筆鋒盡見水墨蒼茫 融入西畫技巧 從傳統中破繭而出〉，《聯合晚報》。

是身外物，並非藝術正道。的確，「水墨」千古事，得失寸心知，歷史自然會為偉大的藝術家們留下名字，無庸爭取。他的創作性格中有堅持的一面，由此可見一般。創作上他以「自在理想主義」為創作宗旨，所言非虛，具體落實他的理念與論述之中。

「不老騎士」的創作理念與論述

藝術家的創作有「兩把刷子」以上，其實所見多有，甚至更多，如「五絕老人」鄭曼青，詩、書、畫、醫、拳皆精。雖然平面，水墨藝術其實是立體式的綜合藝術，詩、書、畫、印就非得俱備一定功力方能成就一張好畫，否則難見於紙面。但若創作者在論述上有一定能量，則另當別論，非得另闢一區討論不可。在臺灣，劉國松、何懷碩、謝里法、林惺嶽、黃光男等等，都是佼佼者。林章湖在大學期間參加詩社又長期自我鑽研，而經年治印又頗有心得，詩書畫印兼佳，無庸置疑，也是「全方位水墨俱樂部」的一員。在筆者與他的談話中，林章湖喜好理論思辨、論述條理有層次、有結構，在我看來是他創作上的極大支撐點。早在 1981 年，他就以〈藝術千秋 人生朝露〉為題抒發藝術職志之觀點：[4]

> 藝術創作歷程，是要耐得住搜盡枯腸與甘為淡泊的種種苦熬，才能在滴滴血汗中綻放豐蘊結實的花朵；一旦，禁不住外在壓力與誘惑，為貧瘠的環境而折腰，為圖名利而寧作諂媚，藝術的種子便隨甜俗而無奈，少有能失而復得。

同時，他也體認到創新的重要性：

> 吸取本身而外的養分以為滋潤、豐蘊，而結合本身精神所在，祈能血肉相融一體，方能盼其有成。

雖然是為畫友而寫，也是自己創作心路歷程上的有感而發吧？另外，也不難發現林章湖的評論能力，相當有深刻見地。他的敢言與堅持，也可見於為學生人物畫展所寫的評論之中：感嘆教條式的山水畫盛行，而人物畫被忽略的困境，並特別強調自然寫生與創作理論並行的重要性。[5] 這是他日後不斷實踐的「二合一」的創作路徑。1991 年的一場臺灣水墨發展座談會，他特別指出：「畫者與論者各執的好比是一體的兩面，雙方如能以同等關心的態度，相互交流激發，提昇層次，則是雙蒙其利。」[6] 他篤行不悖這種理念，且一路走來始終如一。

他對臺灣水墨風格也有定見。他不認為題材或寫生可以完全決定本土性，而是取決於「創作者的價值取向與做法」。臺灣水墨風格其實是風土之下自然凝塑的結果，水到則渠成，毋須強求，反而要與時俱進。他說：[7]

> 期待臺灣風格這個「本土藝術」長久壯闊，就應該落實於文化的融鑄之上，不再自耽於只是純樸的懷舊情結，而忽略了現今社會文化遞變之下應有的應對。古老的農業文明，再也不可能以「懷舊」或「復古」的身段重返，扮演這個現代化社會文化的主流。時代精神應該是發乎自覺自強的意識，能深悟此一文化前途的脈動，自能推動藝術風格早日到來。…一個水墨創作者，如果不從時代文化的角度立命開拓，形成時代的水準與風氣，那我們就無由去質疑目前的處境！

4　林章湖，1981，〈藝術千秋 人生朝露〉，《雄獅美術》130：146。

5　林章湖，1990，〈雲開天青見「人物」─兼談「水墨人物專題展」〉，《雄獅美術》232 期。

6　吳小蕙紀錄，〈「展望臺灣新美術」系列之五 臺灣水墨發展座談會〉，《雄獅美術》246：126。

7　同上註。

「時代精神」一詞源自德文 Zeitgeist，是赫爾德到歌德至黑格爾以來主張不可見但普遍存在於社會特定時空的主宰力量，林章湖年輕時便能體會它的重要性，可見其藝術學之素養。這番語重心長的反思，也在他的創作上反映出來。追求「內省沉潛」的時代創作觀，反對浮面時尚、追捧流行，是他所堅持的對的道路。

以上的想法，隨著閱歷的增長逐漸成熟與體系化，在《自在理想主義－試探水墨藝術的本心畛域》(1997 年) 一書可窺全貌。[8] 這本「知行實證」心得有獨樹一幟的看法，連用語修辭都很特殊。他特別重視「史識」，簡言之，文化演變的軌跡對創作者的影響，因此再次認識歷史、詮釋歷史，從中獲得美學理念作為創作的依據。他提出「深化廣化相對律」的概念，強調內在精神、外在表象的平衡互補，前者指向傳統、後者指向創新。也由此可見，解讀他的創作，從這兩個面相切入是有意義的：[9]

> 深化使創作內涵精神更為深刻豐蘊，耐人尋味；廣化使風格特色更為別出心裁，鮮明超脫。史識能夠穿透時代，使人掌握時代實質意義。透過史識，藝術家適可從容自處於民主社會，以其藝術作為見證。

和「史識」有異曲同工見解的，我印象中是楚戈的「史心」。1981 年，楚戈以另一個想像中的楚戈進行自我對話：[10]

> 我與楚戈為了詩人的「史心」問題在那兒起了爭執。楚戈在談話中突然提到「史心」認為不少現代詩人缺乏回頭看的勇氣，所以在意念中以及作品的表現上，缺乏歷史感，他希望詩人對建立「史心」的問題加以考慮。…我只是認為，這個「史心」的建立，是不是可以廣義的把「現代」也涵蓋在內？因為我覺得在我們身處的時代，有許多事物，如果把它們完好的表現出來，對未來一定具有史的意義，那麼，一個詩人專注於現代精神的刻劃，不也是有一顆「史心」嗎？…就繪畫來說，楚戈對現代詩人的建立「史心」的說法，同樣地可以適用…繪畫的歷史意義，乃至文化精神的延展性，同樣地，是作為現代精神的根基。

英雄所見略同，有歷史感知讓創作有厚度、讓藝術有深度，連結了過去、現在與未來，因此作品的生命會是穿透時空的。總之，再怎麼現代，藝術創作者對歷史與文化縱深有所呼應是很重要的、也是基礎性的，林章湖稱之為「定位」：歷史、文化定位，是文化的根，依此作為自己創作的定位座標。臺灣西畫或水墨創作者，甚至是當代藝術創作者中，強調歷史因素之於創作的重要性（更遑論在地歷史、臺灣歷史）[11]，寥寥數人，他是我見過的倡導者之一。史識觀念的養成，源自他在研究所期間曾修習石守謙的中國藝術史課程，因而體認到歷史觀念之於藝術創作者的重要性。1985 年師大碩士論文《王蒙山水畫風格之研究》便顯示他對史觀之於藝術理解所扮演的關鍵角色。論文摘要開宗明義：「以往研究王蒙繪畫的範圍，大多僅止於概括的敘述與解釋作品，缺乏就畫史觀點來探討其一生繪畫藝術。」[12] 這段說明他的史識奠基軌跡。

8　林章湖，1996，《自在理想主義－試探水墨藝術的本心畛域》。臺北：羲之堂。

9　同上註。

10　楚戈一九八一（楚戈），1981/5/8，〈可以橫絕峨嵋巔〉，《聯合報》。

11　楚戈一九八一（楚戈），1981/5/8，〈可以橫絕峨嵋巔〉，《聯合報》。相關調查，可參閱筆者〈臺灣美術史生態調查的必要性〉，《同心圓：大學臺灣藝術史教師實訪錄》(2018)。臺北：藝術家，頁 4-15。或〈在地與國際：臺灣美術史建構的區域連結〉，《機制‧移行‧內外：重建臺灣藝術史學術研討會論文集》(2019)。臺中：國美館，頁 16-31。

12　https://ndltd.ncl.edu.tw/cgi-bin/gs32/gsweb.cgi/ccd=kmk3MB/record?r1=1&h1=0 [瀏覽日期：2019/11/2]

在創作理念上，林教授也有獨到的「心法」見解：飛相掃心（類似去塵除執的意思）、心法實相（形式與內容的相映）、新法新境（創新技法與題材）、象徵解構（畫面重組等）。可以看出他特別重視創作的心性內省，並轉換成創作的能量；另一方面，他也不排除新的形式、手法與技法，用來反映時代情感。用這一套觀念閱讀林章湖的作品，的確讓人有「心手相印」之密合感，而不只是視覺上面的愉悅而已。「透徹」或許可以用於他對創作的自我期許，這也是他對藝術作為畢生志業的一向執著與堅持：「自在理想主義」一追求自我面貌，抱持一顆赤子之心持續堅持理念。

上面是 1997 年他《自在理想主義》一書的摘述，看來是他創作論述的總結性看法。如果在此處打上句號，也算功德完滿。不料，另一場藝術理論之旅在十數年後展開，讓人再度大開眼界，更印證他對藝術創作上「立論」的高度重視與堅持。

2010 年自臺北藝術大學退休後，林章湖教授效法金庸已近九十之齡完成劍橋大學博士學位，在中央美院攻讀博士學程，最後以《「後現代」與臺灣當代水墨》[13] 論文成為有著教授頭銜之外還加上博士頭銜的藝術創作者。活到老學到老的精神讓人敬佩；他則自嘲自謙是「老來俏」，探論後現代水墨的更是前所未有的「後現代之舉」，只為一償年輕時未了的宿願。把一生黃金歲月貢獻在書畫創作研究與教學，退休後，再來取得藝術博士學位，算是讀「心適」(sim-sik) 的吧？

閩南語「心適」就是有趣、趣味意思，這不就是他所謂的自在理想的意思嗎？看似突兀，實則有跡可循，因為這是他一貫「創作、理論二合一」的進化版：「藝術學術化」，以藝術作為學術之體、學術作為藝術之用。對於創作者是如此，但對於藝術學術工作者的我而言，則體用邏輯可能是相反的「學術藝術化」：以學術作為藝術之體、藝術作為學術之用。創作的主體與學術的主體決定了這種「互為主體」關係，但其極致，可能是互為融入、相互搭襯的無分軒輊境界，路徑不同但殊途同歸。

筆者的博士論文《從深層到表面一現代主義與後現代主義視覺模式研究》[14]（2006 年，臺大社會學研究所）也觸及臺灣後現代視覺文化現象，因此對這本博論特別關注。西方後現代主義的興起大抵上自 1960 年代開始於建築藝術的探討，而 1988 年《繪畫中的後現代主義》[15] 以及李歐塔 (Jean-Francois Lyotard) 的〈後現代狀況〉翻譯與〈臺灣地區後現代狀況及年表初編〉[16]、1989 年《什麼是後現代主義》[17] 的出版，臺灣始進入後現代的討論。接著，隔年陸蓉之出版《後現代的藝術現象》[18] 以及詹明信 (Fredric Jameson) 的《後現代主義與文化理論》[19] 的中文翻譯，臺北市立美術館 1991 年的《現代美術》有後現代藝術座談會的紀錄…開展出「臺灣的後現代狀況」。[20]《什麼是後現代主義》、〈後現代狀況〉與〈臺灣地區後現代狀況及年表初編〉的作者是現代水墨畫家兼詩人羅青。眾所皆知，其水墨作品也帶有濃烈的後現

13　林章湖，2016，《「後現代」與臺灣當代水墨》。新北：花木蘭文化出版社。

14　廖新田，2006 年，《從深層到表面一現代主義與後現代主義視覺模式研究》，臺大社會學研究所博士論文。

15　莫道夫 (Steven Henry Madoff) 著，羅青譯，1988，《繪畫中的後現代主義》。臺北：徐氏基金會。

16　參見《臺北評論》第 6 期。

17　羅青，1989，《什麼是後現代主義》。臺北：五四出版社。

18　陸蓉之，1990，《後現代的藝術現象》。臺北：藝術家出版社。

19　詹明信 (Fredric Jameson)，唐小兵譯，1989，《後現代主義與文化理論》。臺北：合志。

20　鄭惠美整理，1991，〈後現代藝術座談會〉，《現代美術》39：58-63。

代式雜揉風格。這個巧合或許註定了臺灣水墨發展必然和後現代思維結緣（而且和臺灣的西洋繪畫幾乎同步，而非跟隨）。從這個脈絡來看，《「後現代」與臺灣當代水墨》論述的出現並不突兀，而是前後呼應，而林章湖博士當然也把這兩本書列入參考書目，並且也點出臺灣水墨後現代創作與思潮的脈絡，將羅青列入「解構水墨」加以評析：[21]

> 羅青…是臺灣最先公開表名「後現代主義」創作身分，以論述先行的水墨畫家。他擅於援用後現代「拼貼」手法…掌握當代社會信息與現實題材入畫…

在思想體系上，他爬梳西方各大家理論，特別受到高宣揚後現代理論的啟發，因此觀察上更見宏觀視野。總之，這本後現代水墨的研究論著，在兩岸華文世界恐怕都是特殊而有膽識的創舉，同時也完成臺灣後現代水墨論述的架構，可謂集其成者。

林博士以其一生浸淫水墨創作與研究的經歷，探索臺灣水墨後現代現象，在我看來，是他經常強調「筆墨當隨時代」的延續，也是創作實踐與理論思辨的終生實踐。例如，在《馬尾祭》（2012 年）一作中，畫面右黑左白，側面半身自畫像，下有烏鴉三隻，意有所指。後來鳥眼塗上紅藍綠三色，政治隱射之意不言而喻。帶點俏皮反諷的款識如下（底線為筆者所加）：

> 我乃白頭翁，馬尾黑頭鬃，可比後現代，嬌歹［按：美醜，或嬌穠］變猴弄，…

乍看之下，形式上已不太傳統，加上以臺語詩入畫，帶點文人式自嘲，但還沒到後現代的「坎普」愛現程度。「坎普」乃英文 Camp 之發音，假仙誇張、嬌柔造作之意，美國作家、藝文評論者蘇珊桑塔格 1964 年發表《坎普筆記》(Notes on Camp)，從此，camp 就被認定為後現代風格的代表詞。[22]

林章湖的後現代式水墨，並非純西方的後現代徵候，而是開放傳統水墨解構的可能性，[23] 但觀其作品，不論重構、拼貼、或解構者，還是有濃濃的人文底蘊和詩感隱含其內，並非跳梁小丑之無厘頭狀。我認為，他的後現代是經過消化後的後現代，可謂「東方化的後現代」。

端看《「後現代」與臺灣當代水墨》這本論文，其中一章將臺灣當代水墨分成十類，梳理其體系，具宏觀視野，若對一位年輕學者來說都是沉重而艱鉅的任務，更何況是一位退休的資深教授？他是以經驗來承載論述，而應用純粹學理進行辯證，是藝術志業而非沽名釣譽，目的是很「後現代」。

臺灣有「不老騎士」騎重機環島，老人家們騎年輕人的玩意兒哈雷機車，想像那個畫面就很是後現代的違和震撼之感！以此比喻，林章湖可說是臺灣水墨界的「不老騎士」，以傳統水墨素養「馳騁」臺灣的後現代場域，光是這膽識與舉動就讓人佩服不已。以此稱之，是在凸顯他創作態度上「苟日新、日日新、又日新」的求變求新精神，滿載的創作歷程卻有開放自在的豪壯隨時迎接新的挑戰。

---

21 同註 12。

22 參閱郭思妤，2019/5/8，〈史上最難懂的時尚主題！什麼是「Camp 敢曝風」？紐約大都會博物館 "Camp: Notes on Fashion" 展覽揭曉！〉。https://www.shoppingdesign.com.tw/post/view/4133［瀏覽日期：2019/10/28］

23 參閱林章湖，2016，《卅年看山：林章湖書畫展》（彰化生活美學館）自序：「創作精神無不來自時代觀察。自己鑽研後現代水墨議題—似乎，一切既有公式即面臨解構的挑戰。」

章法自在，湖光悠遊

　　林章湖是認真的玩墨者，可謂戲墨人生／人生戲墨的典型。他的風格有的「雄強感性」的組合特質。每一幅作品在造境設景上均力求匠心獨運，且往往有感而發而非為賦新詞強說愁，真誠之情躍然紙上。詩意、感染力與視覺張力之營造濃烈。特別是他的拓法純熟，令人嘆為觀止。筆者曾對臺灣的拓印技法有過發展縱深的耙梳，拙文〈拓印「東方」—戰後臺灣「中國現代畫運動」中的筆墨革命〉[24]發現拓印是戰後臺灣水墨革新運動（或言「新繪畫運動」、「現代中國畫運動」）中現代化、本土化的重要媒介，包括技法與文化意涵雙方面的互文共振。

　　這位「不老騎士」總是讓人驚艷，他開展的山水、人物、花鳥、抽象構成、拼貼與轉折跌宕的書法線條，正是他建立在創作美學理論上的充分藝術實踐。技法上，他強調視覺效果與感受的搭配，並不囿限於筆墨皴染的規制，材質上的運用非常有彈性創意，因此創作主題和表現相當密合，的確有淋漓盡致之感。所發展的各系列，研究琢磨深入，遠觀細賞皆能讓人玩味不已。重視史識與實踐的林章湖博士，一路以來堅持如一，不知不覺地銜接過往臺灣水墨的現代化歷史，並且豪邁地往後現代的道路上揚長而去，在臺灣與華人世界開拓一片華美深邃的「東方後現代」桃花源。

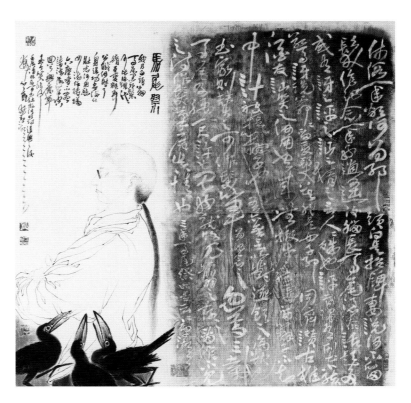

〈馬尾祭〉圖版 p.39

24　廖新田，2019，〈拓印「東方」—戰後臺灣「中國現代畫運動」中的筆墨革命〉，《風土與流轉：臺灣美術的建構》。臺南：臺南市美術館，
　　頁 219-257。

Free Composition, Leisurely Lake:
Dr. Lin Chang-hu's Creative Calligraphy and Painting

Liao Hsin-tien | Director of National Museum of History

The "Free and Ideal" Creative Process

Prof. Lin Chang-hu has shown his unique painting talent since adolescence. His imitation of the traditional ink works are vivid, with the ink colors, composition, and even charm of certain style, which astonishes the viewers and provokes the association that this man is born to take the road and make a living by engaging in it.

As a saying goes, "genius is thirty percent inspiration and seventy percent perspiration." He displays his talent to the fullest, works hard, and strives for improvement. In the junior year of college, he won the third place of the Chinese painting group in the 26th department exhibition of Department of Fine Arts, NTNU (in 1976)(no first prize awarded). The next year, he went further to win the top prize "Award of Minister of Education" in the department exhibition. The work of flowers and birds was highly acclaimed with the comment that "he makes the [egrets] alive with the mature skills."[1] After Lin Yu-shan saw this work, he praised it greatly and believed "Mr. Lin" would achieve something soon in the future. Indeed, dozens of egrets showing their own charm compose a vivid and organic picture. In his later various subjects, he also show the excellent composition ability to bring life to the picture. At the same time, his calligraphy work also won the second prize, indicating his future vantage of excelling in both calligraphy and painting. There was more good news about his art performance. In the graduation exhibition that year, he won the first prize with the work "Egrets," second prize in the calligraphy group, and third prize in the seal carving group. The latter also foreshadows his mastery in seal carving afterwards. This time, he shows the more skillful depicting ability in painting a group of egrets of a larger number, each of which has its special figure and looks vivid. It is as if we could hear the clamor of the chirping assimilated into the dense forest. After graduation, with the excellent performance, he was recommended to join in the competition for the college fine arts awards in the 5th "National Award for Arts" in 1977.

When serving as a teacher, he actively participated in all kinds of exhibitions with great focus and devotion and trained himself through these opportunities. In 1972, he won the second prize of MOE Literature and Arts Creation Awards. In 1975, he won the first prize. In October, 1988, Lin Chang-hu held his first exhibition in Taipei Fine Arts Museum. At that time, his creative concept was reported to be "the 'extra-pattern' of the aesthetic experience and the 'organic structure' related to the contents and forms"[2] as well as the aesthetic height pursued with "ideal" and "expression."[3] This is quite different from the ordinary traditional comments on ink works. (For example, the phrases and citation are both the past regular and standardized viewpoints of painting theories.) What's noteworthy is that it

---

1 Chen Yi-cheng, 1977. "Thousands of Knots in Mind: After Viewing the Exhibition of Department of Fine Arts, NTNU." Lion Art, 73. Note: They should be nightingales.

2 United Daily News, 1988/10/9, P.5. *In Selection of Lin Chang-hu's Paintings*, published that year, there is the interpretation of "extra-pattern" in the preface: to express the feelings with the new skills. "Organic structure" is to emphasize the composition of the momentum.

3 Li Yu-ling, 1988/10/11. "Lin Chang-hu's Brushstrokes in Boundless Ink World: Integration of Western Painting Skills, Breaking out of the Cocoon of Tradition." United Evening News.

is the consensus shared by both him and the ink painters of the new generation that they make innovations bravely without being confined to tradition.

In 1989, the 7th National Art Exhibition held by National Art Museum of China, Beijing, invited Lin Chang-hu, Lin Chang-de, Xiao Jin-fa, Chen Hong-mian, Cheng Dai-le, and Zhang Ke-qin for mutual learning. Lin Chang-hu "accidentally" won the "Youth Prize of Wu Zuoren International Foundation of Fine Arts" with his work "The Fish Against the Turbulent River." The prize was 3000 China Yuans; however, he donated it back to show gratitude to their recognition. The other winner was Wei Ershen, the lecturer of LuXun Academy of Fine Arts (present dean of LuXun Academy of Fine Arts). Wu Zuo-ren made an inscription for the new rising star, "Hua Xiang Liang An (Fragrance across the Strait)," which indicates that his creation strikes a chord with the viewers across the strait. The honor has been regarded as a unique record up to date.

Besides being selected to the literature and arts creation awards, Lin Chang-hu never attends arts competitions. He is given the awards passively instead of striving for them actively. With his full display of talent as a young man, if he had the attempt, he would be quite successful. However, he regards creation as the pure pursuit. Wining prizes in the competitions is additional, not the orthodox way of art. Indeed, ink painting should be a grand business for generations, and the creators are clear about the bitters and sweets in their own mind. History will naturally leave the mark for the great artists. They don't have to strive for it. It can be seen that there is some insistence in his creative personality. In creation, he makes "free idealism" his creative purpose and practices it in his concept and discourse.

The Creative Concept and Discourse of "Dream Ranger"

It is common that an artist has more than two specialties in creation. The number is even larger. For example, Zheng Man-qing, "the old man with five consummate skills," excels in poetry, calligraphy, painting, medicine, and martial art. Although presented on a plane, ink art is actually a 3-dimensional comprehensive art. To create a good painting, there must be certain capability in poetry, calligraphy, painting, and seal carving, or the work can't reach certain level. However, if the creator has the energy to some extent in his discourse, it is another case and has to be discussed separately. In Taiwan, Liu Guo-song, He Huai-shuo, Xie Li-fa, Lin Xing-yue, and Huang Guang-nan are all masters. In college, Lin Chang-hu joined the poetry society and cultivated himself for a long period of time. He also had years of experience in seal carving. There is no doubt that all of these make him excel in poetry, calligraphy, painting, and seal carving and become a member of the "comprehensive ink club." In my conversation with him, I've found that Lin Chang-hu enjoys logical thinking and has levels and structures in his discourse, which are the great support in his creation. As early as 1981, he expressed his viewpoint of making art his career in the article titled "Thousand Years of Art, Morning Dew of Life" :[4]

---

4   Lin Chang-hu, 1981. "Thousand Years of Art, Morning Dew of Life." *Lion Art* 130: 146.

In the creative process of art, one has to endure the hardship of racking his brains and accepting the plainness. Every drop of sweat will give rise to the beautiful flowers and juicy fruit. Once he can't stand the pressure and temptation, surrendering to the barren environment and flattering others for fame and wealth, the seeds of art will wither with the sweet vulgarity and be lost forever.

At the same time, he also realizes the importance of making innovations:

Absorb the external nutrients to nourish and enrich the life and combine them with the personal spirit. The integration of both is expected to achieve something.

Although he writes these words for other painters, he is also expressing his own feelings for the creative process. Moreover, it is evident that Lin Chang-hu's comments are perceptive and insightful. His bluntness and insistence can also be found in the commentaries written for the students' figure painting exhibition. He sighs for the prevalence of the dogmatic landscape painting and the plight of the ignored figure painting and specially emphasizes the importance of paying equal attention to natural sketching and creative theories.[5] This is the "two-in-one" creative path he keeps practicing in the later days. At an ink painting development symposium in 1991, he pointed out: "The painter and the theorist are like two sides of a body. If both can exchange with and inspire each other and upgrade the levels with the attitude of equal concern, that will be a win-win situation."[6] He has been consistent in this idea and stayed true to it.

He also has a fixed opinion on the ink painting style in Taiwan. He doesn't believe that the subject matter of sketching can fully decide the aboriginality. Instead, it depends on "the creator's value orientation and methods." The ink painting style in Taiwan is actually the result naturally formed with the local customs and environment. It is a natural process without any force, and it will also make progress with the time. He said:[7]

If the "local art" of the Taiwanese style is expected to last long and strong, it should be implemented on cultural melting. It should not only focus on the simple nostalgia and ignore the required responses to the dramatic changes in the present society and culture. The ancient agricultural civilization will never return in the form of "nostalgia" or "vintage" and play as the mainstream of the modernized society and culture. The spirit of the time should come from the consciousness of self-reflection and self-reliance, which can help realize the pulsation of the future of the culture and enhance the early arrival of the art style . . . If an ink creator doesn't make explorations from the cultural angle of the time and shape the standard and trend of the era, we have no standpoint to question the present situation!

"Zeitgeist" in German means "the spirit of the times." It is the dominating power that is invisible but universal in

5   Lin Chang-hu, 1990. "Sky Clearing up, 'Figure' Coming Out: On "Ink Figure Painting Exhibition." Lion Art, 232.

6   Recorded by Wu Xiao-hui. " 'Prospect for New Art in Taiwan' Series No.5: Taiwan Ink Painting Development Symposium." Lion Art, 246: 126.

7   Ibid. P.134

the specific time and space of the society, proposed by Herder, Goethe, and Hegel. Lin Chang-hu could understand its importance when he was a young man, which proves his professional literacy in art. The sincere introspection is also reflected in his creation. The creative concept of the times in pursuit of "introspection and pondering" and against the superficial fashion and inflated trend is the right way he insists on.

The thought mentioned above is getting mature and systematic with the increasing experience and presented fully in the book, Free Idealism: An Tentative Discussion on the True Intent and Domain of Ink Art (1997). The book about the "empirical knowledge and action" proposes the unique points of view, and the phrases and rhetoric are special. He pays special attention to "historical concepts," in short, the effect of the traces of cultural transformation on creators. Therefore, there is the need to learn and interpret history again and gain the aesthetic concept from it for the reference of creation. He proposes the concept of "deepening and broadening the relative rule," emphasizing the balance and complementary between the inner spirit and outer appearance. The former means tradition, and the latter means innovation. Accordingly, it is meaningful to interpret his works from the two perspectives.[8]

Deepening makes the creative content and spirit profound, abundant, and intriguing. Broadening makes the style and characteristic unique, vivid, and transcendental.

Historical concepts can penetrate the times and enable people to grasp the real meaning of the times. Through historical concepts, an artist can get along with the democratic society calmly and easily and his art serves as the evidence.

In my opinion, what shares the similar idea with "historical concepts" is Chu Ge's "historical heart." In 1981, Chu Ge did a self conversation with another imaginative Chu Ge:[9]

I had an argument with Chu Ge over the problem of the poets' "historical heart." In our conversation, Chu Ge suddenly mentioned "historical heart," considering that many modern poets lack the courage of looking back. So there is a lack of the historical sense in their thinking and expression of works. He hopes the poets to take into consideration the issue of establishing the "historical heart." . . . In my opinion, is it possible to generally include "modernity" in the establishment of the "historical heart"? It is because I believe if we perfectly express many things in our times, it will be historically meaningful in the future. Then, if a poet focuses on the depiction of the modern spirit, doesn't it mean that he also has a "historical heart"? . . . In terms of painting, Chu Ge's argument of the modern poets' establishing the "historical heart" can also be applicable to . . . the historical meaning of painting and the extension of the cultural spirit, which is similarly the basis of the modern spirit.

Great minds think alike. The historical perception endows the artistic creation with the depth and profoundness,

---

8   Ibid. P.13.

9   Chu He 1981 (Chu Ge), 1981/5/8. "Surpass Ermei Hill," United Daily News.

connecting the past, the present, and the future. Therefore, the life of the works will transcend the time and space. To sum up, however modern the works are, it is essential and basic for an art creator to respond to history and culture. According to Lin Chang-hu, it is called "orientation" : The historical and cultural orientation is the cultural root, with which one can position his creation. There are few people among the creators of western painting or ink painting in Taiwan and even those of the contemporary art emphasizing the importance of the historical factors to creation (not to mention local history, history of Taiwan). However, he is one of the promoters I've seen. The development of the historical concept originates from the course on the Chinese art history he took given by Shi Shou-qian when he studied in the graduate school. Therefore, he realized the importance of the historical concept to an art creator. His master's thesis in 1985, A Study on the Style of Wang Meng's Landscape Painting, shows the critical role the historical concept plays in the understanding of art. The thesis abstract makes a clear statement: "The past studies on Wang Meng's paintings only dealt with the general depiction and interpretation of his works without the discussion on the painting art throughout his life in terms of the historical concept."[10] This explains the trace of the foundation of his historical concept.

In the creative concept, Prof. Lin also has his unique "mental cultivation method" : flying appearance and sweeping mind (similar to getting away from the secular life and obsessiveness), mental cultivation method and true appearance (mutual reflection between form and content), new technique and new level (innovative skills and subjects), and symbols and deconstruction (reorganization of the image). It can be found that he specially focuses on the mental introspection of the creation and transforms it into the creative energy. On the other hand, he is not against the new form, style, and technique, which are used to reflect the emotion of the times. Indeed, with the series of concepts, it is quite pertinent to read and interpret Lin Chang-hu's works, which not only bring the visual pleasure. "Thoroughness" may be applied to his self-expectation toward creation. This is also the consistent attachment and persistence to art as the lifelong career: "free idealism"—pursuing the true self and sticking to the belief with an innocent heart.

The above is excerpted from his book Free Idealism in 1997 and regarded as the summary of his creative discourse. It can be a perfect ending if it is the final chapter. However, another journey of art theory began after more than ten years, which widens our horizon and proves his high emphasis and insistence on "establishing a viewpoint" in art creation.

After he retired from Taipei National University of the Arts in 2010, Prof. Lin Chang-hu followed Jin Yong, who completed the doctorate degree in University of Cambridge at the age of nearly ninety, to study in the PhD program in Central Academy of Fine Arts and finally became the art creator as both a professor and a doctor with the dissertation, 'Postmodernism' and the Contemporary Ink Painting in Taiwan. The spirit of "live and learn" is admirable. He often ridicules himself modestly to be "an ageing swinger," doing the unprecedented "postmodern behavior"

---

10   https://ndltd.ncl.edu.tw/cgi-bin/gs32/gsweb.cgi/ccd=kmk3MB/record?r1=1&h1=0 [Citation Date: 2019/11/2]

of discussing the postmodern ink painting to fulfill the wishes he used to make when young. He has devoted all his golden years to the research and teaching of calligraphy and painting. After retirement, he earned a doctorate degree in art. Isn't this "sim-sik"? "Sim-sik" in Taiwanese means fun and interesting. Doesn't it share the same meaning with his so-called free idealism? It may look abrupt, but there is actually a trace to follow. This is the advanced version of his consistent idea of "the unification of creation and theory," that is, "academic art." Art serves as the body of academic studies, and academic studies can be applied to art. It is true for a creator. However, for me, as an academic worker in art, the logic may be reversed as "artistic academic studies." The academic studies serve as the body of art, and art can be applied to academic studies. The creative subject and the academic subject define the relationship of "mutual subject." To the upmost, it may be a borderless realm of mutual integration and support. The different paths will lead to the same destination.

My dissertation From Depth to Appearance - Visual Models of Modernism and Postmodernism[11] (2006, Department of Sociology, National Taiwan University) also touches the postmodern visual cultural phenomenon in Taiwan, so I have special concern for the dissertation. The rise of postmodernism in the western world approximately started from the discussion on the art of architecture in the 1960s.

In 1988, with the translation of What is Postmodern about Painting[12] and Jean-Francois Lyotard's The Postmodern Condition and the publication of The Postmodern Condition and First Edition of Chronology in Taiwan Area[13] and What is Postmodernism? in 1989, the discussion of postmodernism started in Taiwan. The next year, the publication of Lu Rong-zhi's The Art Phenomenon of Postmodernism[14] and the Chinese translation of Fredric Jameson's Postmodernism and Cultural Theories[15] and the record of the postmodern art symposium in Modern Art of Taipei Fine Arts Museum in 1991 launched the "postmodern condition of Taiwan"[16] The author of What is Postmodernism, Postmodern Condition, and The Postmodern Condition and First Edition of Chronology in Taiwan Area is the modern ink painter and poet Luo Qing. As is known to everyone, his ink works are also infused with the strong postmodern style. With this coincidence, it is destined that the ink painting development in Taiwan will be connected to the postmodern thinking. (And it is almost simultaneous with the western painting in Taiwan instead of following it.) Judging from this context, the appearance of the discourse, 'Postmodernism' and the Contemporary Ink Painting in Taiwan, is not abrupt. Instead, they echo with each other. Indeed, Dr. Lin Chang-hu also includes the two books in his reference list, points out the postmodern creative and thinking context of the ink painting in

11   Liao Hsin-tien, 2006. *From Depth to Appearance: Visual Models of Modernism and Postmodernism*. Dissertation of Department of Sociology, NTU.

12   Steven Henry Madoff. Trans. Luo Qing. 1988. *What is Postmodern about Painting*. Taipei: Xushi Culture and Education Foundation.

13   Please refer to *Taipei Review, Issue 6*.

14   Lu Rong-zhi, 1990. *The Art Phenomenon of Postmodernism*. Taipei: Artist Magazine.

15   Fredric Jameson. Trans. Tang Xiao-bing, 1989. *Postmodernism and Cultural Theories*. Taipei: He Zhi.

16   Organized by Zheng Hui-mei. 1991. "Postmodern Art Symposium." *Modern Art*, 39: 58-63.

Taiwan, and comments on Luo Qing's works by listing them in "deconstruction of ink painting" :[17]

Luo Qing ... is the first to openly express his identity of a "postmodernist" in Taiwan and an ink painter proposing his discourse first. He excels in borrowing the postmodern "collage" technique . . . and gets hold of the contemporary social message and real subject matters in his paintings . . .

In terms of the thinking system, he organizes the major western theories and is specially inspired by the highly promoted postmodern theories. Therefore, he has a grander view in his observation. In sum, the research publication about postmodern ink painting can be taken as the special and bold innovation in the Chinese world across the strait. At the same time, he also completes the framework of the postmodern ink painting discourses of Taiwan by epitomizes all of them.

Dr. Lin explores the postmodern phenomenon of the ink painting in Taiwan with the lifelong experience of indulging himself in the ink painting creation and research. In my opinion, it is the extension of his regular emphasis on "ink and brushstrokes with the times" and the lifelong practice of his creation and theoretical thinking.

For example, in the work "Horsetail Festival (2012)," the picture is black on the right and white on the left. There are three ravens beneath the side bust self-portrait having some special meaning. The eyes of the ravens are painted red, blue, and green, which are the evident political implications. The playful and ironic inscription is as follows (The underlined part is added by me):

I am a Chinese bulbul with the horsetail of black bristle. It is postmodern as beauty and ugliness become tricks . . .At first glance, it is not in a traditional form. Besides, the Taiwanese poem in the painting with some of the literati's self mocking does not reach the "camp" level in postmodernism. "Camp" denotes "ostentatious, exaggerated, affected, and theatrical." The American writer and art critic Susan Sontag published Notes on Camp in 1964. Since then, "camp" has been tied to postmodernism.[18] Lin Chang-hu's postmodern ink painting is not the pure western postmodern style but the open possibility to deconstruct traditional ink painting.[19] However, whether it is reconstruction, collage, or deconstruction, his works have the strong humanistic heritage and poetic feeling instead of the incoherent nonsense. In my opinion, his postmodernism is processed by him and can be called "oriental postmodernism."

In the dissertation 'Postmodernism' and the Contemporary Ink Painting in Taiwan, one of the chapters classifies the contemporary ink painting in Taiwan into ten categories, organizing its system with a grand view. It is a heavy

---

17 Ibid 12, P.68.

18 Please refer to Guo Si-yu, 2019/5/8. "The Fashion Most Difficult to Understand Ever! What is 'Camp?' The Metropolitan Museum of Art "Camp: Notes of Fashion" Unveils!" https://www.shoppingdesign.com.tw/post/view/4133 [Citation Date: 2019/10/28]

19 Please refer to Lin Chang-hu, 2016. Thirty Years of Mountain Viewing: Lin Chang-hu's Calligraphy and Painting Exhibition. (National Changhua Living Art Center) Preface: "The creative spirit always comes from the observation of the times. As far as my personal research on the postmodern ink painting issue, it seems that every existing formula is facing the challenge of deconstruction."

and arduous task for a young scholar, not to mention for a retired senior professor. He carries on the discourse through his experience and applies t he pure theories to deal with the speculation. It is the career of art instead of the pursuit of reputation. The purpose is "postmodern."

In Taiwan, the "dream rangers" ride their motorcycles to travel around Taiwan. Imagine that the old men ride the Harley Davidson motorcycles which are supposed to be ridden by young men. The picture is postmodern, fresh and shocking! Lin Chang-hu can be regarded as the "dream ranger" in the ink painting world of Taiwan, speeding through the postmodern field of Taiwan with the traditional ink literacy. With the courage and action, he is admirable. This comparison is to highlight his creative attitude and the spirit of making new explorations each and every day. The creative process is loaded with the open and free magnificence ready to meet the new challenges anytime.

Free Composition, Leisurely Lake

Lin Chang-hu is a serious ink player, a representative who has been playing ink games throughout his life. His style is a combination of "majesty and sensitivity." In every work, he spares no effort to pursue the unique craftsmanship in creating the scene and atmosphere. He tends to express his feelings spontaneously rather than pretentiously. Sincerity is vividly revealed on the paper. The strong poetic feeling, appeal, and visual tension are created. In particular, his skillful rubbing technique is breathtaking. I have had a deep exploration and organization of the development of the rubbing techniques in Taiwan. In my article, "Rubbing the 'East' : Ink Revolution of 'Modern Chinese Paining Movement' in Postwar Taiwan,"[20] it is found that rubbing is the important medium of modernization and localization in the revolutionary movement of ink painting in Taiwan (also called New Painting Movement or Modern Chinese Painting Movement), including the intertextual resonance of both techniques and cultural meanings.

The "dream ranger" always astonishes people. The composition of landscape, figures, birds, flowers, and abstraction and the calligraphic lines of collage, transition, and freedom are his full art practice in the creative aesthetic theories. In terms of techniques, he emphasizes the combination of visual effects and feelings without being limited by the wrinkling and dyeing standards of ink painting. In terms of the material application, he is very flexible and creative, making the creative subject and performance close to each other and expressed to the fullest. The different series of works developed by him are worth deep research and exploration. Whether appreciating them at a distance or taking a closer look, a viewer will find the everlasting fun and meaning from them. Dr. Lin Chang-hu, who puts emphasis on the historical concept and practice, has been persistent all the way, unconsciously connecting the history of ink painting modernization in Taiwan, imposingly heading toward the path of postmodernism, and cultivating a beautiful and profound "eastern postmodern" Xanadu.

---

20   Liao Hsin-tien, 2019. "Rubbing the 'East': Ink Revolution of 'Modern Chinese Painting Movement' in Postwar Taiwan." *Local Culture and Transformation: The Construction of Fine Arts in Taiwan*. Tainan: Tainan Art Museum. P.219-257.

"潛龍勿用"的後現代變法

林章湖｜潛龍居士

回想九歲開始學習書畫，至今已過了半個世紀，恍如一瞬，前塵如煙，心中百味雜陳，難以言喻。也許早就命中註定，當我在澳底福隆那少年十載，於先父庭訓下寫帖臨畫的傳統基礎冥冥之中已決定了我的一生。也沒料到如今自己藝術會走向「後現代」變法之路。

天道酬勤，讓我當年就讀師大美術系，系展與畢業展接連獲得國畫第一名肯定，雖然體認詩書畫印等傳統工夫是創作養分，而科班教育更讓我了解理論與創作同樣重要，尤其在於體認「時代精神」做為真正創作前提。因此，我認為從傳統邁向現代，唯有開放自我胸襟，才能筆墨當隨時代以拓展自我藝術境地。

服務於風氣前衛的臺北藝大，將近三十年的教學相長之下，「自在理想主義」成為我書畫創作的美學境界。我沉潛探討自主自足的藝術語言，取各家之長，融鑄己法乃至為法，具現真實可讀的筆墨風格，反映自我審美境界與意義。天地大美，靈犀會心俯拾皆是，多年來舉辦個人書畫展，積累了不少主題系列，無不徜徉於自在本心，追撫理想，包含了田園雪衣的鷺鷥，逆境求生的游魚，關渡櫛沐的風情，飫遊胸懷的山河，難得糊塗的解構，憧憬故事的物語，退休歲月的舒懷，禪法詩意的書藝篆刻等系列作品。

面對 21 世紀自由開放的藝術潮流，已是全球化影響之下的「後現代」，臺灣仍充斥西方論調，尚未是臺灣民主社會多元藝術文化共融的「當代」，而書畫界始終敬而遠之，相對也失去了與當代精神對話的契機。回顧我個人曾經在「自在理想主義」中出現「糊塗系列」的解構水墨，說明自己從當代思潮中借鏡取法已行之有年了。因此，丹青不知老之將至，我退休後毅然研究「後現代」，出發點即在正面探討自我藝術與當代交鋒的問題，這就彷彿白石老人當年「衰年變法」為自己打通任督二脈的作法一般。當然，鐘鼎山林，其中冷暖如人飲水罷了。

顛覆性的「後現代」話語權出自當代西方，其理論固然十分複雜，言人人殊，但是東西方有些思想道理其實是異曲同工。譬如古聖先賢的典故可謂不勝枚舉：佛家「鏡花水月」、莊子「無用之用」與東坡「反常合道」等乃東方「後現代」傳統思維的端倪；草聖張旭濡髮狂書，米元章以蔗渣代筆作畫，而文人畫史中詩、書、畫、印在絹紙上隨機混搭，這些屬於東方「後現代」手法，只是不同時空下各自有解讀意義而已，歷史本身即是古為今用取之不盡的文化智慧。雖然當代藝術無不追求突破，但終非一昧向西方看齊。綜觀後現代正銜接著現代容顏，並迴盪著古代跫音，同時也浮現未來身影，而其本身自由潛伏的能量造化，就端視個人的運用之妙了。

所以，一切法為我所用，研究並創作「後現代」，是我個人整體藝術生命修行的一道法門，取之從我，非我從之。我的《後現代與臺灣當代水墨》博士論文，試圖以畫史觀與風格論闡述「傳統」、「現代」與「後現代」彼此交輝的自我創作經驗，同時自我蠡測其未來展望與價值。至今白頭赤子與「後現代」交戰之下，這回展覽的水墨作品〈神話之鳥〉、〈永憶江湖〉、〈留住傘洲〉、〈魚躍龍門〉、〈關渡行舟〉、〈無用大用〉、〈西藏秘境〉、〈小隱〉與糊塗系列等；書藝作品〈謙卑之最〉、〈陋室銘〉、〈後現代〉、〈文化花瓶〉等，乃至篆刻〈少水魚〉、〈君子不器〉、〈酒歡伯〉、〈壺 HUGO〉等在破立兼容，正反辯證的解構思維中，從容彰顯東方「後現代」的另類人文意指與興味。

茲拈句一首聊發心中幽思〈我觀後現代〉：

百年翰墨花非霧，後現多元石破驚。解構流行孰治本，無明省悟任掇英。

行舟浪險猶心證，舞劍圖窮尚制衡。莫信全球歸一的，無涯理境策前程。

時代浪潮無不考驗創作者的智慧，藝術真理永遠在彼岸。易經有句話：「潛龍勿用」，隱喻世事適機而用，用意在審慎運用罷了。這恰好可提醒自己投身「後現代」變法，要知所取捨進退，而後亦應作如是觀。我自臺北藝大退休十年，得於中山國家畫廊殿堂展覽，喜出望外，以「後現代」變法視角，盤點心路歷程與回顧創作願景，深感榮幸與惶恐，尚望各位前輩先進同道不吝批評指教。

　　藉此，首先感謝當代著名書藝家、國父紀念館館長梁永斐先生邀請與館內同仁協助，前臺灣藝大校長黃光男博士，史博館館長廖新田博士，與臺灣師大教授白適銘博士分別撰寫專文介紹，亞洲大學游明龍講座教授設計畫冊，以及義之堂廖建欽及陳筱君賢伉儷慨然撥冗策展，一路情義相挺。承蒙這些學者專家老友們的鼎力襄助，以及借畫的諸多單位、藏家的共相盛舉，實在令我感銘於心，謹合十致謝。

　　僅以此次展覽獻給在天之靈的先父。

〈後現代〉局部 圖版 p.134

The Postmodern Transformation of "Hidden Dragon, Do not Act"

Lin Chang-hu | Lay Buddhist Qianlong

In retrospect, I started to learn calligraphy and painting when I was nine. Half century has passed in a flash. The dreamlike past memories are the ambivalent and indescribable feelings in heart. Maybe everything is predestined. The childhood years in Audi and Fulong and the traditional foundation I laid when my late father instructed me in calligraphy and painting have unwittingly decided my life. I didn't expect that my art will transform into the "postmodern" style.

God rewards the diligent. When I studied in Department of Fine Arts, National Taiwan Normal University, I won the first place of the Chinese painting group in the department exhibition and graduation exhibition. I realize that the traditional skills of poetry, calligraphy, painting, and seal carving are the creative nutrients. However, the professional training has made me understand that theory and creation are equally important, especially in terms of the understanding that "the spirit of the time" should be the real creative premise. Therefore, I believe that when moving toward modernity from tradition, only by opening our own mind can we raise the personal art level in ink painting with the time.

I served in the avant-garde school of Taipei National University of the Arts and benefited from my teaching for nearly thirty years. "Free idealism" has become the aesthetic level of my calligraphy and painting creation. I am indulged in exploring the independent and self-sufficient art language, integrating the specialties of each school into the personal law, presenting the real and readable ink style, and reflecting the personal aesthetic level and meaning. The beauty of the earth is everywhere in mind with the tacit understanding. In the past years, by holding the personal calligraphy and painting exhibitions I have accumulated many topics and series, which wander with a free mind and recall the ideals, including the series works of snowy white egrets in the field, swimming fish struggling for life, windy and rainy charm of Guandu, magnificent landscape, blissfully ignorant deconstruction, stories of prospect, leisure of the retired years, calligraphy and seal carving of the Zen and poetic style.

Facing the free and open art trend in the 21st century, "postmodernism" under the influence of globalization, Taiwan is still full of the western views and hasn't come to the "contemporary time" with the diverse art and cultural integration in the democratic society. The calligraphy and painting circle has been stayed far away from it and therefore lost the chance to converse with the contemporary spirit. In retrospect of my deconstruction of ink painting in "blissful ignorance series" of "free idealism," I have learned from the contemporary thinking for years. Therefore, neglecting my old age, I determined to study "postmodernism" after retirement. The intention is to directly discuss the issue of the encounter between personal art and contemporary art. This is similar to Qi Baishi's "old age reform," which turned over a new leaf to his personal conception. Indeed, there is no accounting for taste as only the wearer knows where the shoe pinches.

The subversive "postmodern" proposition comes from the contemporary western world. The theory is indeed quite complicated, and the different theories have the different interpretations. However, the eastern and western worlds actually share some similarities in thinking. For example, there are countless allusions of the ancient sages: the Buddhist "flowers in a mirror and the moon's reflection in water," Zhuangzi's "the usefulness of the useless,"and Su Shi's "breaking rules but following reasons" show the clue of the eastern "postmodernism." The wild calligraphy written with wet hair by the sage of cursive script, Zhang Xu, Mi Yuan-zhang's painting with sugarcane bagasse, and the casual combination of poetry, calligraphy, painting, and seal printing on silk paper all belong to the eastern "postmodern" skills. There are the different interpretations and meanings in the different time and places. History itself is the endless cultural wisdom as the ancient experience can be borrowed and used in modern time. The contemporary art has to pursue breakthroughs, but it does not mean following the western world all the way. As a whole, postmodernism connects the modern style, echoes with the ancient footsteps, and at the same time shows the future looks. How its free hidden energy is expressed depends on the personal application.

Therefore, I can apply all the laws to study and create "postmodernism." It is the approach of my personal overall art life practice. I don't follow it; instead, it comes from me. My dissertation 'Postmodernism' and the Contemporary Ink Painting in Taiwan attempts to elaborate the personal creative experience of a combination of "tradition,""modernism," and "postmodernism" from the viewpoint of painting history and with the style theories and at the same time speculates on the future prospect and value. After my argument with "postmodernism," I present the ink paintings of this exhibition including "Bird of a Legend," "Forever Memory," "Keep Sanzhou," "Fish Leap over Dragon Gate," Guangdu Boat Cruise," "Great Use of the Useless," "Secret Land in Xizang," "Small Hidden"and the Blissful Ignorance Series. The calligraphy works include "Ultimate Modesty," "Epigraph in Praise of My Humble House," "Postmodernism," and "Vase of Culture." The seal works include "Less Water Fish," "The Accomplished Scholar is not a Utensil," "Joyous Drinking Uncle," and "Pot HUGO." These works are to make breakthroughs and compatibility and composedly manifest the alternative humanistic meaning and interest in the deconstructive thinking of dialectics.

I've written a poem, "My Opinion on Postmodernism," to express my inner thought:

The hundred-year ink art is like flowers in the mist.

Postmodernism is so shockingly diverse.

Deconstructing the fashion is the fundamental cure.

After worries and reflection, pick the essence at will.

The dangerous waves on a boat journey are the clear understanding in mind.

Encounter them with the dancing swords and sharp knives.

Don't believe in the universal truth for the world.

The future should the endless process of reasoning and manifestation.

The waves of the time are always testing the creators' wisdom. The truth of art always lies on the other side. As *I Ching* said, "Dragon is lying in Wait." It suggests that the things in the world have to be used carefully in the proper time. This reminds me that I have to know when to advance and when to retreat when engaging in the "postmodern" changes and follow this concept hereafter. After I retired from TNUA ten years ago, I am overjoyed to hold an exhibition at Chungshan National Gallery. From the perspective of "postmodern" transformation, I have look back on the journey of my hearts and my creative prospect. With a deep feeling full of honor and prudence, I expect the seniors and art lovers to share their opinions with me.

Here I'd like to express my gratitude to the contemporary famous calligrapher, director-general of National Dr. Sun Yat-sen Memorial Hall, Mr. Liang Yung-fei, for his invitation and to the staff of the hall for their assistance. The former president of National Taiwan University of Arts, Prof. Huang Guang-nan, the director-general of National Museum of History, Dr. Liao Hsin-tien, and the professor of National Taiwan Normal University, Dr. Bai Shi-ming, write the introduction articles for me. The chair professor of Asia University, You Ming-long, designs the album for me. The couple Liao Jian-qian and Chen Xiao-jun of Xi Zhi Tang spare their time to plan the exhibition. They have supported me all the way. The generous assistance of these scholars, experts, and old friends and the full support of the units and collectors lending out the paintings touch my heart. I express my sincere gratitude here.

I'd like to dedicate the exhibition to my late father in heaven.

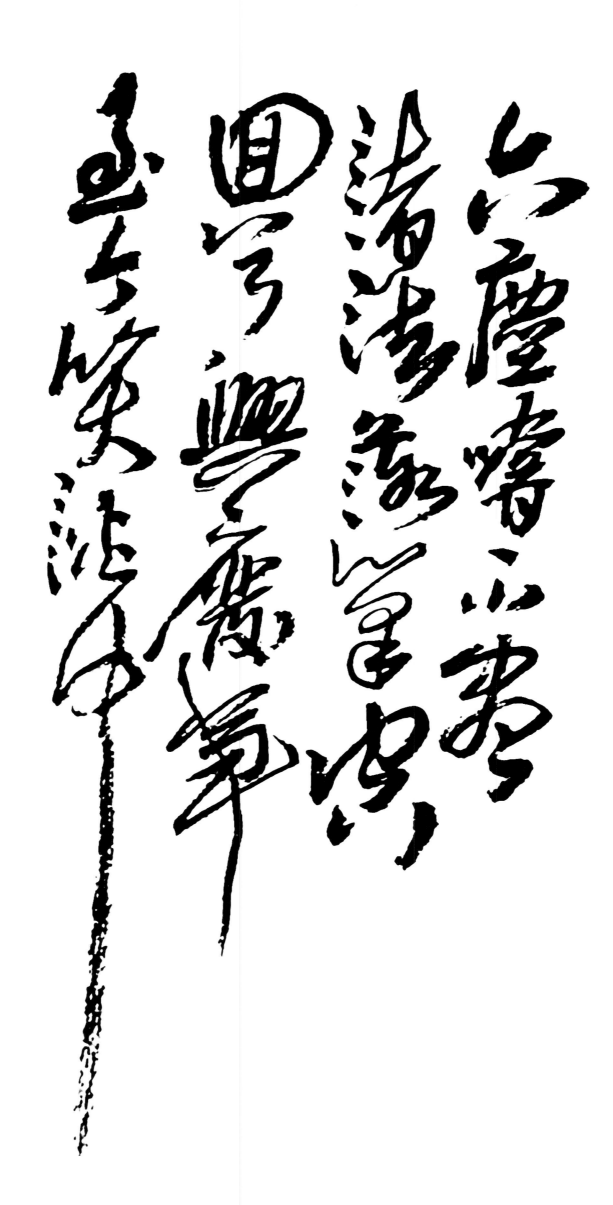

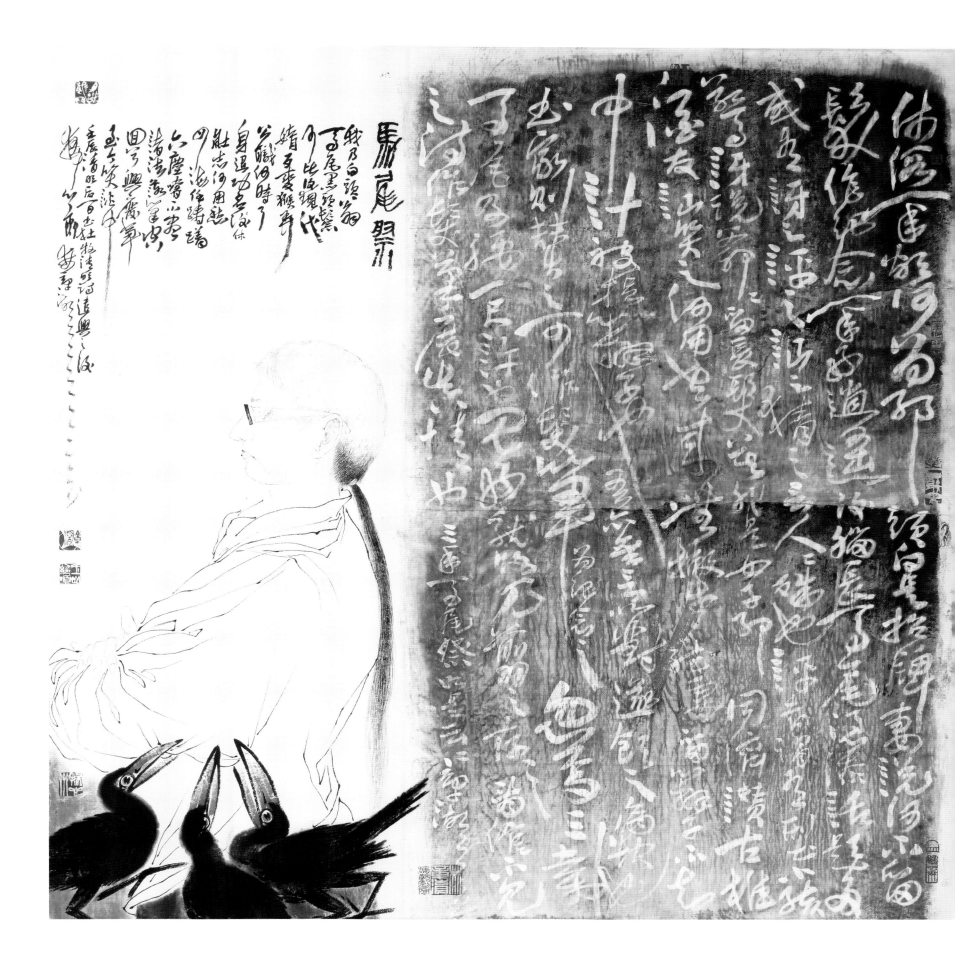

馬尾祭　123×123 cm　2012　畫家自藏
Story of Ponytail

馬尾祭（篆）。

我乃白頭翁，馬尾黑頭鬃，可比後現代，嬉耍變猴弄，公職何時了，身退功名休。

壯志何用愁，四海任躊躇，六塵嗜不盡，諸法落筆空，回首興廢事，至今笑談中。壬辰清明后一日書杜牧清明詩遣興之後，掃心齋林章湖。

休假一年欲何為耶，（餘略）。

〈羊〉〈白髮三千丈〉〈投石射鬼〉〈龍〉〈象〉〈掃心齋〉〈酒歡伯〉〈林章湖〉〈吃飽剩鬧〉

〈魚躍龍門〉〈章湖雙魚〉〈玉山絕頂〉〈掃心齋〉

臨張大千秋壑鳴泉（14 歲） 95×35 cm 1968 畫家自藏
Salute to Chang, Da-Chien

秋壑鳴泉，戊申年臘月林章湖十四歲寫于雙中二戊。
〈林章湖印〉

臨唐伯虎草堂清話（15 歲）131×66 cm 1969 畫家自藏
Salute to Tang, Bo-Hu

貢寮源遠出雙溪，水秀山明景物齊，茅舍松陰甘淡泊，春風桃李自成蹊。
章湖賢契畫囑為題句，浙東韓玉梁。己酉年桂月粵棉林章湖十五歲寫。

〈樂〉〈韓玉梁〉〈人生如夢夢如人生〉〈林章湖印〉

白鷺圖　240.8×118.4 cm×2　1977　國立臺灣師範大學典藏　畢業美展國畫第一名
Egrets

丁巳初夏，林章湖。

〈林印〉〈章湖〉

大地徜徉 23×68 cm×4 詩塘 16.5×68cm 1990 畫家自藏
Wander of Egrets in Wild

大地徜徉（篆）。三百五十年前，苦瓜僧嘗言我用我法，允為治藝至言。究其真義乃謂窮一己之心，運用之妙。故妙用全視個人蒙養之功。今日藝術理念追求日　，無不標榜風格特色，此絕非一家言者流可同日而語。今人不重一心妙用，奢言興革，豈不罔然。

〈庚午〉〈車馬喧室〉〈林章湖畫〉〈羊〉〈己巳〉〈章湖〉
〈庚午〉〈林章湖畫〉〈車馬喧室〉
〈庚午〉〈章湖〉〈己巳〉〈羊〉〈章湖〉
〈庚午〉〈章湖〉〈己巳〉〈章湖〉

風竹白鷺　134×69 cm　1983
Family of Egrets　畫家自藏

癸亥年青陽端月，章湖於塗城（土城）。

〈林印〉〈章湖〉〈清源山客〉〈真意忘言〉

幽居賦閒白鷺影 180×90 cm 1983
County Sight of Egrets 畫家自藏

幽居賦閒白鷺影。憶寫楊梅所見鷺群印象，
癸亥夏月，章湖並記於臺北土城。
〈林印〉〈章湖〉〈車馬喧室畫印〉
〈章湖翰墨〉（程代勒刻）

清流圖卷 48×356 cm 1995 國立臺灣美術館典藏
Clear Stream

清流源本，合污下焉，奮進尚志，莫使墜之深淵也。弗逆自性，得見心境。
乙亥梅月望後一日，章湖感記，無住生心齋雨窗。

〈食氣〉〈林印〉〈章湖〉〈飛相掃心〉

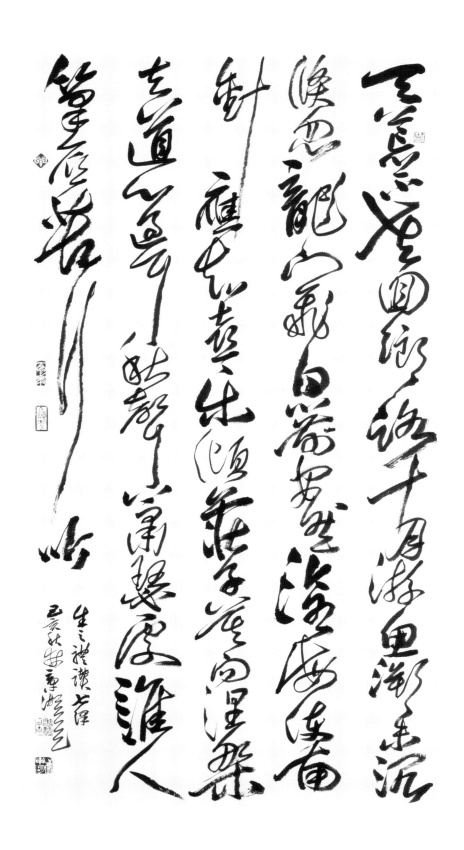

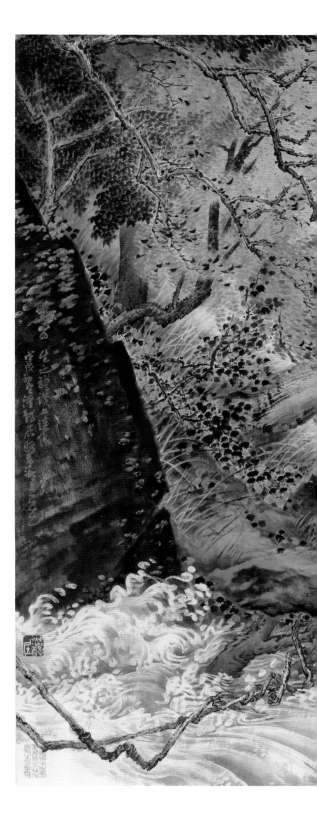

生之禮讚二連作 121×553 cm 含題詩 2018 畫家自藏
The Ceremony of Life

生之禮讚（篆）。

冰河暖化，改不了返鄉的印記；

水壩顧頇，擋不了洄游的鬥志。

一泓清流，載沉著億萬年不止嘆息，生命原是悲欣交集，一場淒美無悔的祭禮。

丙申九月暮秋雨復秋虎，掃心齋，林章湖。

〈林〉〈章湖〉〈一片冰心〉〈真放精微〉〈丙申〉〈大象無形〉〈掃心齋〉〈筆歌墨舞〉

生之禮讚二連作，戊戌初冬潛龍居，林章湖。

〈白頭赤子〉〈戊戌犬〉〈林印〉〈章湖〉〈潛龍居〉〈無事忙中老空裏有哭笑本來沒有我一切皆可拋〉

天荒不老回鄉路，十月游魚洄未沉。倏忽龍門飛白箭，安然滄海使南針。

應知喜樂傾莊子，莫問涅槃去道心。過耳秋風蕭瑟處，誰人筆底苦行吟。

生之禮讚七律，己亥秋，林章湖。〈天聽〉〈羊〉〈一念三千〉〈白頭赤子〉〈潛龍居〉〈林章湖〉

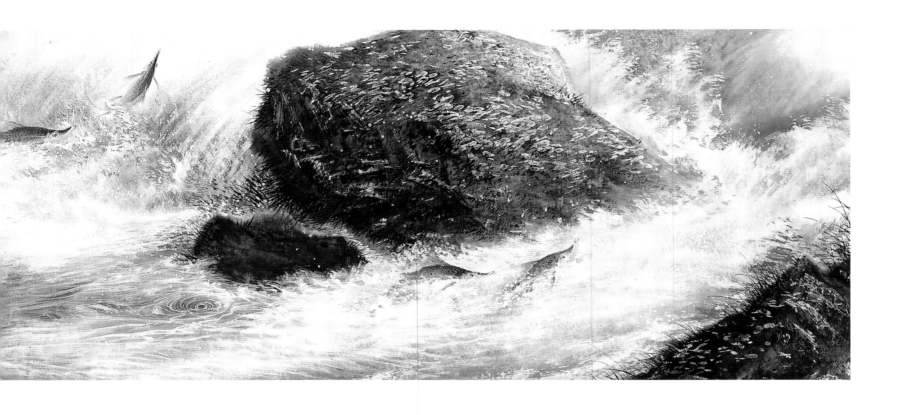

生之祭　136×70 cm　2010　私人收藏
Ceremony of Life

生之祭（篆）。觀鮭魚之迴流，體生物本命之無執，命之鼓息，一路誓死不悔，
淒美之極。色相皆空，流水與歸之。庚寅正月初九，掃心齋鐙下並記，寒流窗外。
章湖。
〈林印〉〈章湖〉〈魚躍龍門〉〈千錯萬錯〉〈掃心齋〉

上善若水　48×178 cm　2017　私人收藏
Kindness

上善若水（篆）。
上善人緣廣，茶香遠客歡。九如新意畫，古董舊時觀。
若水銀刀躍，其昌五世蟠。指南山翠綠，福地子孫冠。
吾嘗以礬膠畫游魚之趣，已成自家心法，此寓老子上善若水之境，拈詩並題。丁酉夏至，掃心齋林章湖。
〈林印〉〈章湖〉〈掃心齋〉〈赤子心〉〈祥〉〈白頭赤子〉〈雞大吉〉

上善若水之境，指詩華題「上善若水」，揮毫凝意源，吾嘗以礬探畫魚游之趣，已筆色寫活地寫於水，指南此翠一綠福物，一泰源，古墨蘸時寫觀深水銀刀體，其昌五之傳，兰善人緣際椎若遠宗乾九出新童畫

躍魚圖　137×68 cm　1990　畫家自藏
Sparkling Fishes

躍魚圖（篆）。庚午仲夏，章湖寫于車馬喧室。
〈林章湖〉〈湖羊〉〈清源山朝客〉

七家灣流金　98×123 cm　2019　畫家自藏
Formosan Landlocked Salmon

七家灣流金（篆）。己亥夏，潛龍居章湖。

〈豬〉〈大象無形〉〈林章湖印〉

臺灣究竟古流金，封陸櫻鮭絕壑深。望海迢迢終不濟，冰河難忘溯初心。
己亥初夏拈句億載初心一首，潛龍居炎窗鐙下林章湖。

〈林印〉〈章湖〉〈歲月靜好〉〈一念三千〉〈五風十雨〉〈七家灣〉

小谿之晨 68×68 cm 1988 臺北市立美術館典藏
Morning at creek

小谿之晨·章湖作以銷暑氣也。〈林〉

阿里雲意 93×90 cm 1983 私人收藏
Mist in A-Li Mt.

一九八三年歲在癸亥秋虎，章湖作阿里雲意於臺北塗城（土城）。

〈林印〉〈章湖〉〈水窮雲起〉〈車馬喧室〉

驚嘯圖　154×84 cm　1988
Howling Wave　私人收藏

驚嘯圖（篆）。憶昔年少隨父客次，
三貂灣瓦楊之居，風雨來犯，門檻嗄
嗄，屋漏滴盆。浪聲哄哄，如隔窗外
擾人清夢。倏忽十有五載，今復觀焉
別有一番滋味，狂風排浪，白波走雷
電，黑霧藏魚龍，此余稱北海景觀之
雄奇者也，異乎落日歸漁，海市燈火，
溫和之貌者也。昔者為困頓之所蔽
也，今者心性之所嚮也。蓋事過境遷，
情亦隨之變耳，而人生際遇若煙海放
舟載浮沉，得失如幻似真，焉能得之
心而忘機耶？感懷繫之，因以圖記。
民國七七年歲在戊辰小暑，章湖並識
于車馬喧室炎窗下。

〈林印〉〈章湖〉〈車馬喧室〉

漁村舊事 96×34 cm 1987 台灣創價學會典藏
Fishing Village

漁村舊事（篆）。丁卯深秋，章湖追寫。

〈林印〉〈章湖〉〈真意忘言〉〈晨夕素心〉

秋牧圖 69×68 cm 1989 私人收藏
Pasture in Autumn

秋牧圖（篆）。己巳歲暮・章湖・車馬喧室記之。
〈林印〉〈章湖〉〈車馬喧室〉

玉頂彤雲　138×70 cm　2009　畫家自藏
Red Cloud of Jade Mountain

玉頂彤雲（篆）。
強登玉峰氣自豪，杉柏雲海風蕭蕭，
紅塵素心消迷藏，秋高浮鳶寄九霄。
己丑清明后數日，章湖，掃心齋晴牕。
〈林印〉〈章湖〉〈己丑牛〉〈忘機〉
〈滄海一粟〉〈掃心齋〉

旭日翔鷗　136×68 cm　2017　畫家自藏
Flying Seagulls at Sunrise

嶔峨鐵壁豬涯跡，旭日狎鷗任自飛。
俯瞰龍宮驚墨客，方覺景勝復迷離。
七絕一首題之，章湖又識。
臺灣馬祖東引安東坑道寫生之作。
丁酉春，林章湖。
〈林印〉〈章湖〉〈羊〉〈雞丁酉〉〈掃心齋〉

洞天雨燕　137×69 cm　2019　畫家自藏
Swallows in Taroko

鴻蒙太魯不知春，鬼斧中橫泣山神。
一線洞天餘雨燕，淙淙漱玉絕風塵。
太魯閣峽谷乃天地間之一大奇觀也。今吾飽覽
目遇神會，若將心入畫腕底飫遊之，亦何斤斤
於胸竹耶？此中印證石濤所云山川為吾代言，
然焉。己亥夏五月潛龍居炎窗下，林章湖。拜
觀故宮張大千蘇花公路一卷，氣勢磅薄逼人，
可否借膽於萬一，又識。
〈浮雲〉〈林印〉〈章湖〉〈一念三千〉
〈潛龍居〉〈忘機〉〈湖曠〉

浯島風神 34×137 cm 2019 私人收藏
Wind Lion

浯島風神（篆）。

明鄭砂吹虐，獅爺請鎮風。猙容慇復笑，法力備無窮。

敵我觀天幻，邪正恃神忠。浯州烽火遠，永樂已相融。

重題舊句。乙未夏隨廖修平院長赴金門寫生，嘗云風獅爺分公母，公者葫蘆示之，母者愛心示之，誠為藝術之一別解，不禁令人會心一笑耳。

今屬吾寫之，茲錄為助興焉。己亥初夏潛龍居，林章湖。

戴冠茲為勝，飛翎頂上風。登科官帽羽，耀祖狀元公。

浯島功名錄，翰林世代封。文星傳稗史，瑞兆喜相通。右題金門戴勝一首。

〈林章湖〉〈潛龍居〉〈五風十雨〉〈道法自然〉〈畫中有詩〉〈大吉大利〉

戴冠花為猴飛絕細頂之鳳光出科官帽羽耀祖狀元浩湯島功名錄轎亭戊戌代封受書畫譚史瑞兆吉祥相画

右郭年門

戴勝写

滌襟圖 123×123cm 2018 畫家自藏
Overlook

滌襟圖（篆）。戊戌冬雨，潛龍居士並詩，林章湖。

滄溟風獵獵，東引滌吾襟。入耳鷗聲近，回神谷道深。

天王學目望，紫氣下巖侵。猶勝徐霞客，蓬萊一日尋。

〈潛龍居〉〈林印〉〈章湖〉〈壺 HUGO〉〈白髮三千丈〉〈君子不器〉〈赤子心〉〈五風十雨〉

五臺雲腳 90×96 cm，詩塘 23×90 cm 2014 私人收藏
Wu-tai Mountain

問道無心，甲午，章湖。〈常想一二〉〈象〉〈林章湖〉

五臺雲腳（篆）。五臺山乃文殊菩薩勝地也，文殊主智慧學問功名，以白獅座騎，法相莊嚴。己丑炎夏雲腳至此，心中但願佛法與畫法會通，
庶幾筆下一切法可為己法，歸來日久遂釀此心境也，唯同行好友克齊兄代勒知之。甲午端午後一日，掃心齋主林章湖。

雲腳問道謁五臺，一夜文殊破壁來，夢醒沈浮身幻影，今生頓悟出塵埃。

章湖又識。

〈林章湖〉〈湖師〉〈飛相掃心〉〈千錯萬錯〉〈一念三千〉〈顛倒夢想〉〈掃心齋〉

海神石俑　150×180 cm　1995　私人收藏
Stone Forest

海神石俑（篆）。自古人與天爭，莫知天之不可欺。驚石林奇觀，
誠造化神工之極矣，景奇故境亦勝焉，人何得而爭之耶？
海神獨造群俑，莊嚴肅然，怎奈隻手直落，亦稱佳想否。章湖並記
於無住生心齋。
〈林印〉〈章湖〉〈無住生心齋〉

隱遯歲月　70×138 cm　詩塘　34×138 cm　2012　畫家自藏
Years of Retirement

滄泊生涯（篆）

白髮早生早退休，往事付之流水東，冷軒伴我老學童，隱遯歲月多滄泊也，又識。甲午炎夏六月，林章湖。〈象〉〈一片冰心〉〈水窮雲起〉〈滄海一粟〉〈羊〉〈林章湖雙魚〉

隱遯歲月（篆）。船之為漁家維生之載具，猶如文人筆墨之於功名也。今日世事炎涼本無奇，然而幾番翻騰，吾誠感時不我予，我亦不與時也。必也識時務隱遯江湖，以為縱浪大化馳騁萬里，吾生有涯，藝海無涯，憶昔風光逝者如斯如斯。人生行舟至此，所當止罷了，還我真如，信乎此生歲月之所終也。福建惠安斑駁老漁船寫生得稿，筆墨抒懷略寫心境耳。壬辰夏，掃心齋晴窗下，章湖。

〈龍〉〈林印〉〈章湖〉〈一片冰心〉〈忘我〉〈掃心齋〉

白林翱鷹　137×70 cm　1987　畫家自藏
Hovering Eagle over the Forest

一九八二年三月下旬，遊美北往長木公園途中，見平野白林無際，春寒撲面一片蕭索，為之觀止。今追寫之，恐去當時遠矣。民七六年春，章湖。

〈林印〉〈章湖〉〈車馬喧室〉

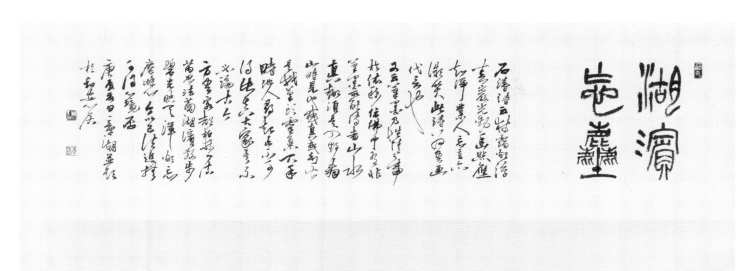

湖濱忘塵 56.5×83 cm 詩塘 24×83cm 1999 私人收藏
Along the Quiet Lake

湖濱忘塵（篆）。石濤詩云：林藹欲浮春，巖光動幽照。應知淨業人，忘言亦微笑。此詩為吾畫代言也。（中略）方吾客都柏林芮思法蘭，
湖濱散步，碧光映天，渾欲忘塵滌心。今以己法追撫可得心境否？庚午夏日，章湖並題於和安心居。

〈林印〉〈章湖〉〈浮雲〉

湖濱寂寂，興來獨往，水鷗不見，誰與話舊。己卯之春月，章湖客思筆墨。

〈林章湖〉〈客愛一年〉

三明治時光　55×97 cm　2005　台灣創價學會
The Sandwich Time

三明治（篆）。吾客都柏林，攜一塊三明治渡一個午後時光。公園獨自徜徉，金秋滿地，真人生逍遙。章湖追寫於和安心居炎窗下。
此作與己卯《秋韻》同工異曲，吾愛秋意紛披，輒令游客渾忘歸期。客居簡樸，然逸趣自在自得，二〇〇五年八月一日並記之。

〈林章湖〉〈客愛一年〉〈拈花〉

翡翠金秋　69×95 cm　2013　私人收藏
Irish Bright Autumn

翡翠金秋冷蕭蕭，筆底繽紛夢中飄，十五寒暑空回首，最憶世紀老酒槽。
吾初訪愛爾蘭設計學院，薛瑞頓院長見面即倒一杯威士忌，歡迎吾遠來客座，莫怪乎院中留有三百年威士忌酒廠，乃酒文化古今相傳也。
今追寫聊記美談。癸巳秋颱天兔方離，掃心齋，林章湖。

〈顛倒夢想〉〈林章湖〉〈客愛一年〉〈一片冰心〉

石窟庵　88×96 cm　2016　私人收藏
The Cave Buddha

石窟庵（篆）。韓國慶州吐含山千年石窟庵乃有唐宗教藝術一脈也，吾佛莊嚴慈悲，如沐法喜殊勝焉。為之詠：

東海迎日雲吐含，頑石成佛洞成庵，山谷演音松護法，普露眾生日月年。

丙申吾客座東大，隨依恩法師恭謁之，歸來數日落筆寫之。掃心齋林章湖。

〈林印〉〈章湖〉〈一片冰心〉〈一念三千〉〈白頭赤子〉〈飛相掃心〉〈無住〉

寒英 89×96 cm 2019 畫家自藏
Cherry Blossoms in Winter

寒英（篆）。客座傳真法，冰心悟覺章。春花飛逝者，白髮散清狂。
丙申客座韓國東國大學，春櫻繽紛夢中常見，今追寫之。己亥秋日潛龍居晴窗下拈句並題，林章湖。

〈林印〉〈章湖〉〈歲月靜好〉〈道法自然〉〈白頭赤子〉〈迷花〉

諸法無相（雞）50×200 cm 1994 高雄市立美術館典藏
No Phase

諸法無相（篆）。藝其唯心造也。諸法非相，相之非者不泥於相，實相也。相者五蘊之端倪也，法者一心之修行也。師而無師，能致無住而生其心，
自具法度，可謂得心法致實相矣。若倒技為藝，著相失心，昧相妄法，不復言也。吾嘗苦思心造，今馭法以超相，若之行深，亦感佛前掃心之困頓也。
甲戌夏五月端午後一日，章湖並記於無住生心齋。

〈林印〉〈章湖〉〈湖羊〉〈十年格物〉

刣豬公 96×60 cm 1994 畫家自藏
Festival

刣豬公。舊年三月廿三土城迎媽祖刣豬公。神農宮鬧熱滾滾，豬公陣十幾隻，看起來真徜徉。豬公攏嘛比大隻，
聽講市內少人飼豬，就開錢去庄腳買人飼便的，有法度拜大豬公，面子卡要緊，神明繪講話，請採就好。

這擺迎媽祖，豬公上重壹仟玖佰貳拾斤，主人攔是民意代表，莫怪真臭揚，有錢好辦歹（代）誌。聽講刣大豬公
會當保庇賺大錢，毋知有影無？阿湖畫了憚寫。

〈林印〉〈章湖〉〈甲戌〉〈生長於斯〉〈無住生心齋〉

池中魚　138×69 cm　2019　畫家自藏
Catching the Fishes

池中魚（篆）。
世變天機分五葉，陳家三代聚埕池。
齊心涸澤銀刀窟，涉足撈鮮散食頤。
可嘆雲煙無片瓦，徒憐田鶯點山眉。
當年稚子何追憶，夢裏囊中寫未遲。
憶昔兒時承天路外祖陳厝涸池捉魚印象，今追寫
拈詩並記。己亥新月春雨方歇，應土城桐花節，
潛龍居士林章湖。

〈林印〉〈章湖〉〈五風十雨〉〈赤子心〉
〈白頭赤子〉〈歲月靜好〉〈如少水魚〉
〈潛龍居〉〈噍飽剩閒〉

拈華圖　138×69 cm　2018　畫家自藏
Tung Blossom

拈華圖（篆）。
清源英落猶禪意，隱密山門洞世機。
勸俗捨緣宜信早，求生念佛莫遲疑。
飄飄法雨波羅密，瀟盡人間剎那時。
諸漏肉身常苦惱，老僧隨喜拈花倪。
土城家鄉首開桐花節風氣之先，迄今廿二載矣。
清源山桐花三月雪已蔚為勝景也。昔時吾佛說
法，迦葉拈花微笑，今時廣公上人想當然耳。虛
擬作之並題七律一首，以為戊戌桐花節之說項，
然否。丁酉隆冬寒流窗外，清源山客林章湖。
萁萌露濕遊人徑，一季桐花穀雨神。
瀟向青山無寒客，來往自在覺吾身。
復拈一絕，擱筆又記。
〈忘機〉〈羊〉〈真意忘言〉〈林印〉〈章湖〉
〈浮雲〉〈歲月靜好〉〈清源山客〉〈潛龍居〉
〈如少水魚〉

日月桐修　138×69 cm　2017　畫家自藏
Practice of Monk

日月桐修（篆）。

清源日月禪房寂，落雪桐花法雨飄。

念佛餐風僧度眾，蓬萊小乘載今朝。

釋廣欽上人渡臺肇庭承天禪寺於土城清源山，
苦修於天上山日月洞也。上人弘法渡化眾生，
勸人一心念佛，不食人間烟火，水果充饑，故
人稱水果師。吾出生於清源山下外祖陳家，幼
年即瞻上人法相，幸霑法喜，印象歷歷如昨
也。今桐花節聯展乃寫此略錄因緣耳。丁酉春
雨寒流，掃心齋居士林章湖。

〈無住〉〈忘機〉〈一片冰心〉〈林印〉〈章湖〉
〈羊〉〈滄海一粟〉〈掃心齋〉〈忘我〉

善惡之戰　45×127 cm　1994　畫家自藏
The Fighting between Kindness and Evil

世態炎涼，人性詭譎，不禁令人悵然，徒呼可恨可恨。觀印尼峇里島峇隆與讓特善惡交戰不絕，不得不畫之。甲戌冬十一月，章湖。

〈林印〉〈章湖〉〈飛相掃心〉

伏虎調心　137×63 cm　2016　私人收藏
Practice of Buddhist

伏虎調心（篆）。自古畫虎尤難，難在於不得寫生故也。
史之禪畫者如牧谿殆由臆想致之。吾師玉山仙早年師承扶
桑堂本印象水墨寫生，乃傳統之正脈而獨創一格也。畫虎
筆勢猶如庖丁解牛，而骨氣精神無不全矣。欲使山君阿堵
炯炯儼人，未嘯而風生，此獨絕處無人能出其右也，故世
人樂道，論諸當代稱之為伏虎師並無不可。典型夙昔，知
之者易而畫之者難，今試撫之，直令吾等小子望虎興歎
耳，略記緬懷之。
丙申初春正月寒流驟外，掃心齋主林章湖。
〈十年格物〉〈掃心齋〉〈無住〉〈飛相掃心〉
〈顛倒夢想〉〈真放精微〉
〈一片冰心〉〈丙申〉〈林印〉〈章湖〉

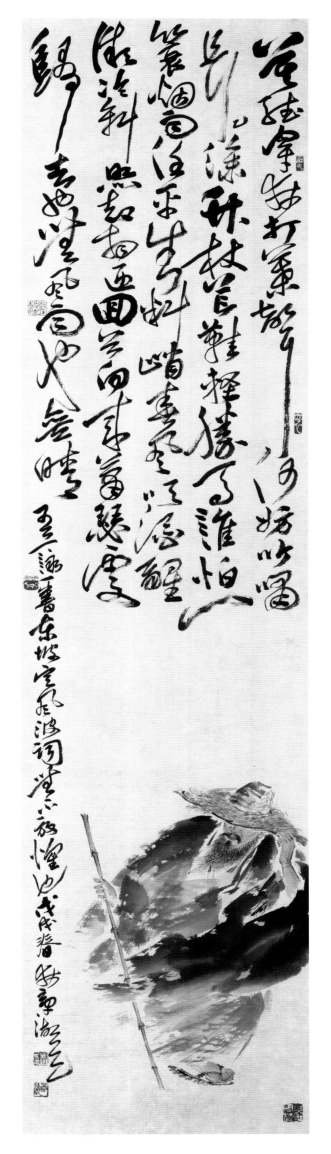

歸去（東坡）137×34 cm　2018　畫家自藏
Dong-Po

莫聽穿林打葉聲，何妨吟嘯且徐行。竹杖芒鞋輕勝馬，誰怕？一蓑煙雨任平生。
料峭春風吹酒醒，微冷，山頭斜照卻相迎。回首向來蕭瑟處，歸去，也無風雨也無晴。
吾一詠一書東坡定風坡詞無不放懷也，戊戌春林章湖。

〈浮雲〉〈赤子心〉〈歲月靜好〉〈戊戌犬〉〈林印〉〈章湖〉〈水窮雲起〉

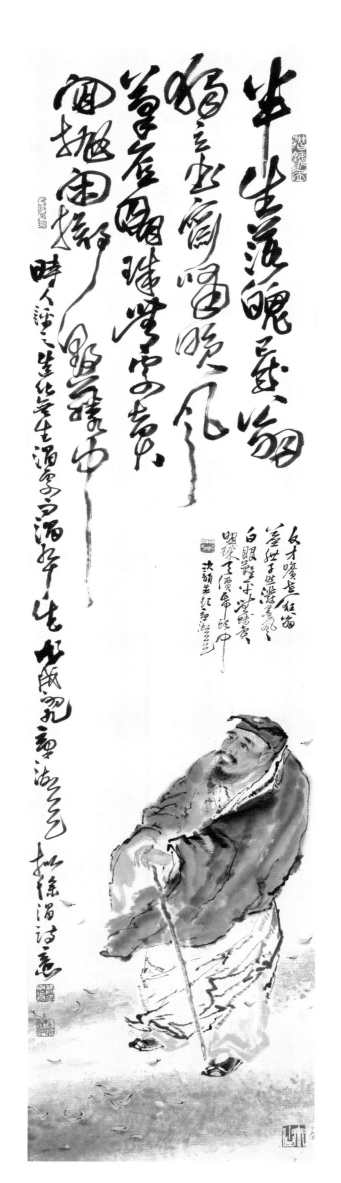

晚嘯（徐渭）137×34 cm 2018 畫家自藏
Xu-Wei

半生落魄已成翁，獨立書齋嘯晚風。筆底明珠無處賣，閒拋閒擲野藤中。
文才曠世一狂翁，塵絕子然潑墨風，白眼難平無睱賣，明珠天價紙頭中。次韻並題，章湖。
時人評之：造化無生渭處而渭卒生。戊戌初九，章湖擬徐渭詩意。

〈潛龍居〉〈戊戌犬〉〈無住〉〈千錯萬錯〉〈林章湖印〉〈在山泉清〉

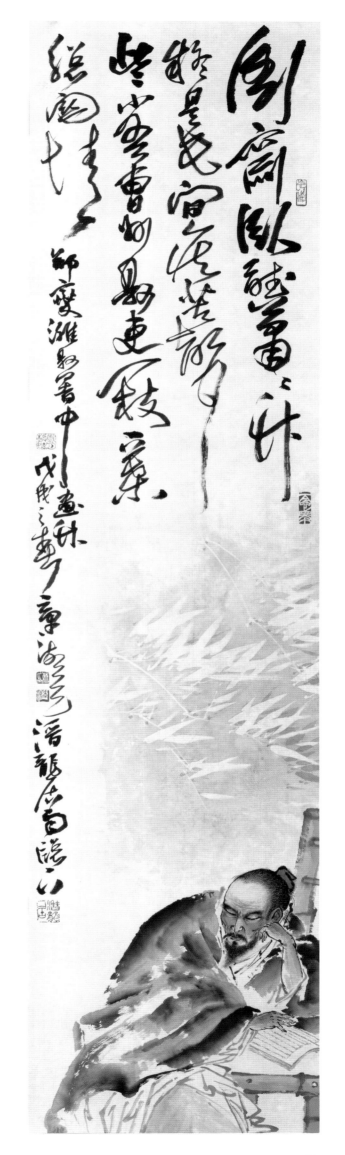

臥聽（板橋）137×34 cm 2018 畫家自藏
Zheng Ban-qiao

衙齋臥聽蕭蕭竹，疑是民間疾苦聲。些小吾曹州縣吏，一枝一葉總關情。
鄭燮縣署中畫竹，戊戌之春章湖潛龍居雨窗下。

〈忘機〉〈一念三千〉〈歲月靜好〉〈林印〉〈章湖〉〈潛龍居〉

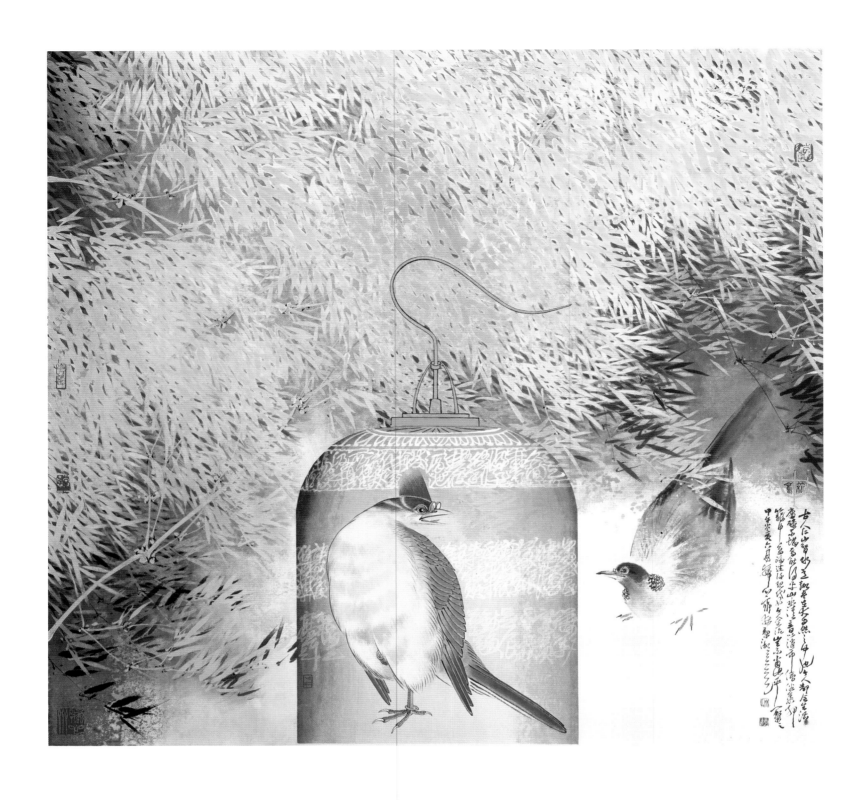

籠中鳥 90×96 cm 2014 私人收藏
Caged Bird

籠中鳥（篆）。古人仁山智水，意趣盡在大自然之中也。今人都會生活庸碌不堪，焉能得乎山水清音，以消市儈俗氣耶？籠中鳥論述後現代也，
今人生活豈不肖此乎？一粲之。甲午炎夏六月，掃心齋林章湖。
〈林印〉〈章湖〉〈雙鵲京喜〉〈忘機〉〈常想一二〉〈掃心齋〉〈瑤林仙館〉

食祿觀　180×90 cm　2012
畫家自藏
Views on Preserving Health

食祿觀（篆）。俗話説民以食為天
也。人不分賢愚富貴，而食有豐薄
之別，富豪之家口含金湯匙一食千
金；貧苦之家則柴米油鹽必也計較，
此先天食錄無由更之，然則後天食
祿何由得益之？吾自以為持之養生
為重，斟酌各人體質而定食定量，
新鮮清淡，享之色香美味，節之口
腹暴食也。但循養生之道，自然長
保健康自在，得展我長才伸藏於
世，此道不啻臻於人生真正價值之
良方也。誠為放諸四海皆準之時代
食祿觀也。
吾生有涯，吾藝無涯，但持之觀省
自惕之，借十鷺用載畫意也。壬辰
新春伊始，章湖，掃心齋晴窗下。
〈忘我〉〈噍飽剩閒〉〈雙鵲京喜〉
〈象〉〈龍〉〈雙魚林章湖〉
〈掃心齋〉〈顛倒夢想〉〈飛相掃心〉
〈真放精微〉。

湖心島　34×135 cm　2004　畫家自藏
Island in Lake

湖心島（篆）。西藏巴松湖之湖心島，島上主奉琳瑪派蓮花生大師，謂男女雙脩，寺外置生殖器（木材）供人膜拜，堪稱一大殊景也。
依舊稿寫之存之。甲申之夏六月，民國九十三年七月二十九日於和安心居晴窗下。吾有幸得師言復得師筆墨，西藏之行焉復何求之耶？
允為珍念之。忽忽二年已過，吾師耳提面命，終得懸之於院長辦公室，他日見此必不以怪吾怠慢之。善禧師賜吾號章措，刻之並鈐之以
證之。丙戌夏識。〈浮雲〉〈林印〉〈章湖〉〈羊〉〈章措〉

不到西藏旅遊，安知高原之上猶有湖山似江南。林芝又譽謂雪域江南。甲申七月，善禧時在林口。（餘略）
〈鄭〉〈善禧〉〈羊〉〈趙仁多吉〉

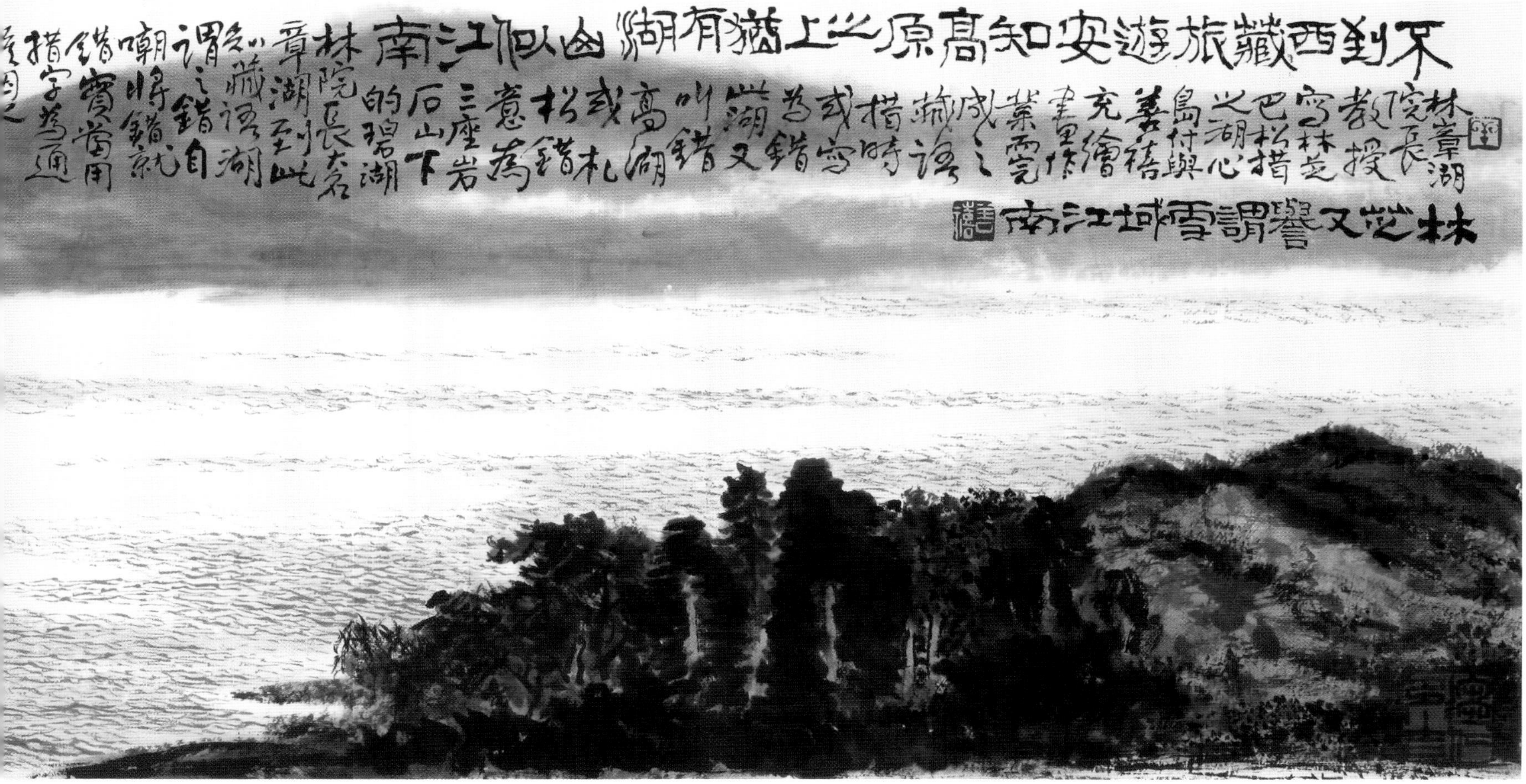

月光歸牧　68×68 cm　2016　畫家自藏
Returning Sheep in Moonlight

月光歸牧（篆）。丙申炎夏，應新疆國畫院邀請寫之並記，林章湖。
此吾一九九一年暑遊絲路火州所見光景也。趕著羊兒踏著月光，落筆之際，彷彿王洛賓小小羊兒要回家歌聲響之耳邊，不禁憧憬也。
章湖又記。

〈林章湖〉〈掃心齋〉〈忘機〉〈湖師〉〈道法自然〉

雪中寶舟 70×69cm 2016 私人收藏
Tibet Yaks in Snow

雪中寶舟（篆）。西藏四千米高原但見牦牛不畏風雪，喻之寶舟，亦吾佛加持使之然也。
丙申炎夏追寫，林章湖。

〈在家出家〉〈冷暖自知〉〈林印〉〈章湖〉

寒川　88×96 cm　2019　畫家自藏
Glacier

互古冰川洌，寂寥黯碧穹。飛鴻千里遠，不見落霞紅。
冰川非常見故難致之，塗抹略得不似之似，其趣端在一己意象耳。己亥秋暮潛龍居，林章湖。

〈林印〉〈章湖〉〈湖師〉〈潛龍居〉〈君子不器〉〈渾金〉〈在家出家〉

藏春　89×97 cm　2019　畫家自藏
Spring

藏春（篆）。潛龍猶未醒，雷雨滌封塵。撲面雲初散，林芝綠似春。
西藏舊遊始知雪域林芝綠如江南春，吾未曾或忘焉，漫記之。無法之法寫之亦稱秘境也。林章湖。

〈日日新〉〈林印〉〈章湖〉〈翠竹法身〉〈潛龍居〉〈忘機〉〈放下〉〈一年三千〉

秘境 88×96 cm 2019 畫家自藏
Mystery

遊目天山外，放懷六合時。歸人無半語，唯有筆頭知。

一己之法得與西藏秘境神合，不知何法何境何人使之然，亦不得人解也。己亥夏潛龍居林章湖。

〈林章湖畫〉〈白髮三千丈〉〈潛龍居〉〈五風十雨〉

神話之鳥　48×180 cm　2009　畫家自藏
The Bird of Myth

神話之鳥（篆）。鳳頭燕鷗是謂之也。

鳥嶼無人鳥自在，天堂鳳鷗真自然，昨日神話今日空，爲唱環保不問天。

己丑初秋，章湖拈句並題。

〈己丑牛〉〈日日新〉〈羊〉〈浮雲〉〈千錯萬錯〉〈顛倒夢想〉〈滄海一粟〉〈章湖雙魚〉

神韵鸟心

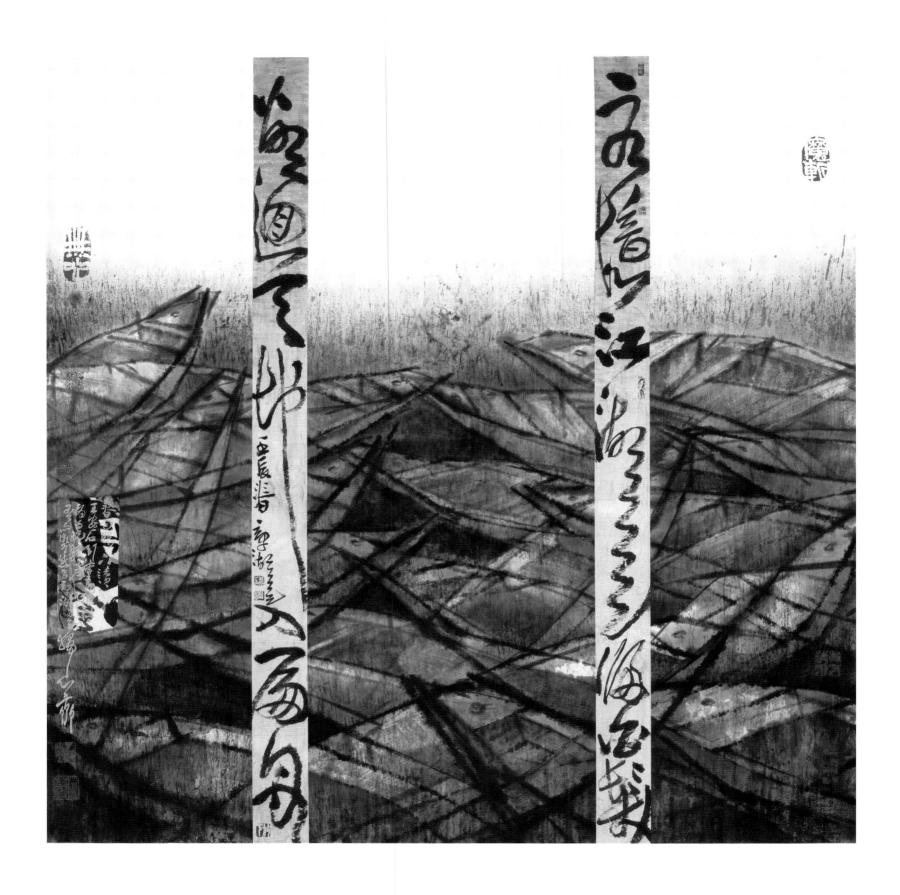

永憶江湖 123×123 cm 2012 私人收藏
Reminiscent

永憶江湖歸白髮，欲迴天地入扁舟。壬辰春，章湖。

〈浮雲〉〈象〉〈龍〉〈林印〉〈章湖〉〈放下〉

春雨窗下，讀王安石引李商隱詩為自況心境也，吾亦頗有感焉。章湖，掃心齋。

〈魔斬〉〈真放精微〉〈投石射鬼〉〈無心〉〈顛倒夢想〉〈滄海一粟〉〈掃心齋〉〈魚躍龍門〉〈掃心齋〉

留住傘洲 123×123 cm 2012 私人收藏
Sandbank

留住傘洲（篆）。潮神堆沙一傘洲，渺渺波臣嘶竹寮，昔日榮景今安在，只有迎風鷗逍遙。

臺灣外傘頂洲乃海中移動之島，前屬雲林，近乎嘉義東石也，真滄海桑田之變幻也。吾去春登臨攬勝，此作追寫奇觀天工神韻之一二耳。

辛卯冬章湖，掃心齋晴窗下。東石外傘頂洲之夜，辛卯暮冬寒雨初歇，章湖。

〈林印〉〈章湖〉〈羊〉〈浮雲〉〈白髮三千丈〉〈嘵飽剩閒〉〈顛倒夢想〉〈掃心齋〉〈章湖雙魚〉〈忘我〉

魚躍龍門 70×138 cm 2012 私人收藏
Proceed to success

龍門心法（篆）。魚躍龍門今何在耶？魚非魚，門非門，龍門在心中，不得言說，可得心處亦為殊勝。吾拈廢紙誑作龍門心法耳，
識者笑之。章湖，壬辰之春，掃心齋廬下。

〈林章湖〉〈放下〉〈忘我〉〈龍〉〈千錯萬錯〉〈掃心齋〉〈噍飽剩閒〉〈魚躍龍門〉〈真放精微〉

小隱　69×68 cm　2016　畫家自藏
Seclusion

小隱（篆）。己法上法，吾試新法新境之旨也，筆底山居遠離塵囂炎涼，此中雖非大隱之志而識者幾希？丙申夏六月，掃心齋林章湖。

〈一片冰心〉〈白髮赤子〉〈林印〉〈章湖〉〈掃心齋〉

樂在糊塗 180×96 cm 2017
Muddle 畫家自藏

為官唯恐聰明不，鄭燮糊塗獨悟知。
但念心安因退讓，非圖福報大無私。
丁酉秋高拈詩喻之，林章湖。
鄭板橋先生難得糊塗，允為後人處世
之至理名言也。吾一介退士所為何事？
窗明几淨，若得糊塗真意，隨手寫去，
樂在其中，焉計工拙，滿紙壺圖何妨
亦作解套耳，知我者一粲可也。丁酉
白露後潛龍居，章湖。

〈林印〉〈章湖〉〈潛龍居〉〈酒歡伯〉
〈噍飽剩閒〉
〈白髮三千丈〉〈豬行路〉〈白髮赤子〉
〈章揩〉〈忘我〉
〈千錯萬錯〉〈丁酉〉〈放下〉〈羊〉
〈投石射鬼〉

金糊塗　96×180 cm　2016　畫家自藏
Muddle

世事真真假假，台語金即是真，吾試金畫壺圖，可謂金糊塗也，又為難得糊塗之一別解，然否？丙申初冬，章湖。

糊塗之至，吾令之亂法無法之法，己法亦法是謂之後現代顛倒夢想也。章湖識。

〈林章湖雙魚〉〈掃心齋〉〈魔斬〉〈羊〉〈無住〉〈豬行路〉〈羊〉〈穿石〉〈道法自然〉〈酒歡伯〉〈顛倒夢想〉〈筆歌墨舞〉

111

十年磨劍 69×138 cm 2018 畫家自藏
Immortal Preparation

十年磨一劍，霜刃未曾識。今日把示君，誰為不平事。
吾作壺圖已過廿三寒暑之久，雖不止十年磨劍之功，今得引詩以弭糊塗習氣，亦得斬不平事於一二，呵呵一粲之，章湖潛龍居雨窗並題。
〈白頭赤子〉〈冷暖自知〉〈十年格物〉〈穿石〉〈一念三千〉〈嘸飽剩閒〉〈白髮三千丈〉〈羊〉〈顛倒夢想〉〈羊〉〈如少水魚〉〈戊戌〉
〈雞大吉〉〈湖曙〉〈無住〉〈潛龍居〉

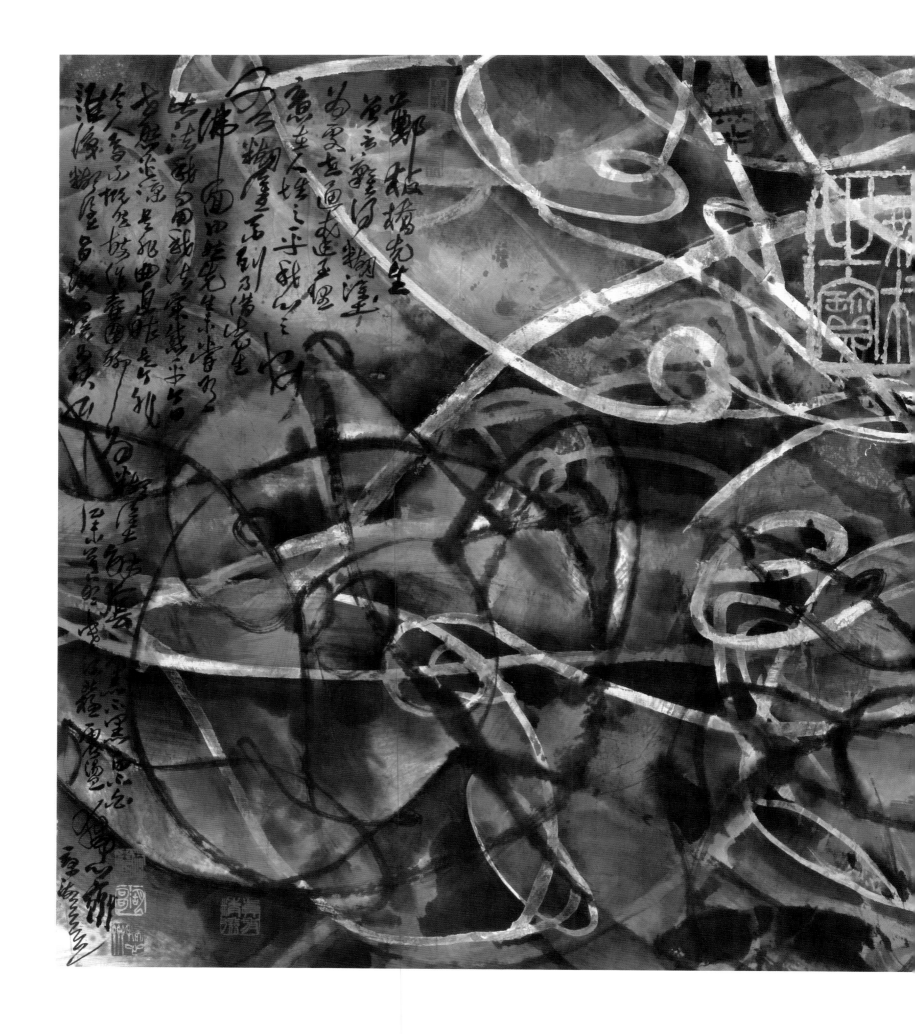

糊塗無極　96×180 cm　2016　畫家自藏
Muddle

鄭板橋先生曾云難得糊塗，為處世通達至理，意在人性之平，我心之安。吾糊塗系列乃借先生佛面也，然先生未嘗有此法，我自用我法，
實感於世態炎涼，是非曲直昨是今非，令人焉不慨然，故作壺圖聊為糊塗解套。黑不黑，白不白，誰識糊塗旨趣？自娛為快耳。乙未暮冬，
寒流北極震盪，掃心齋章湖。

〈林章湖〉〈湖哥〉〈掃心齋〉〈真放精微〉〈酒歡伯〉〈投石射鬼〉〈筆歌墨舞〉〈糊塗無極之寶〉

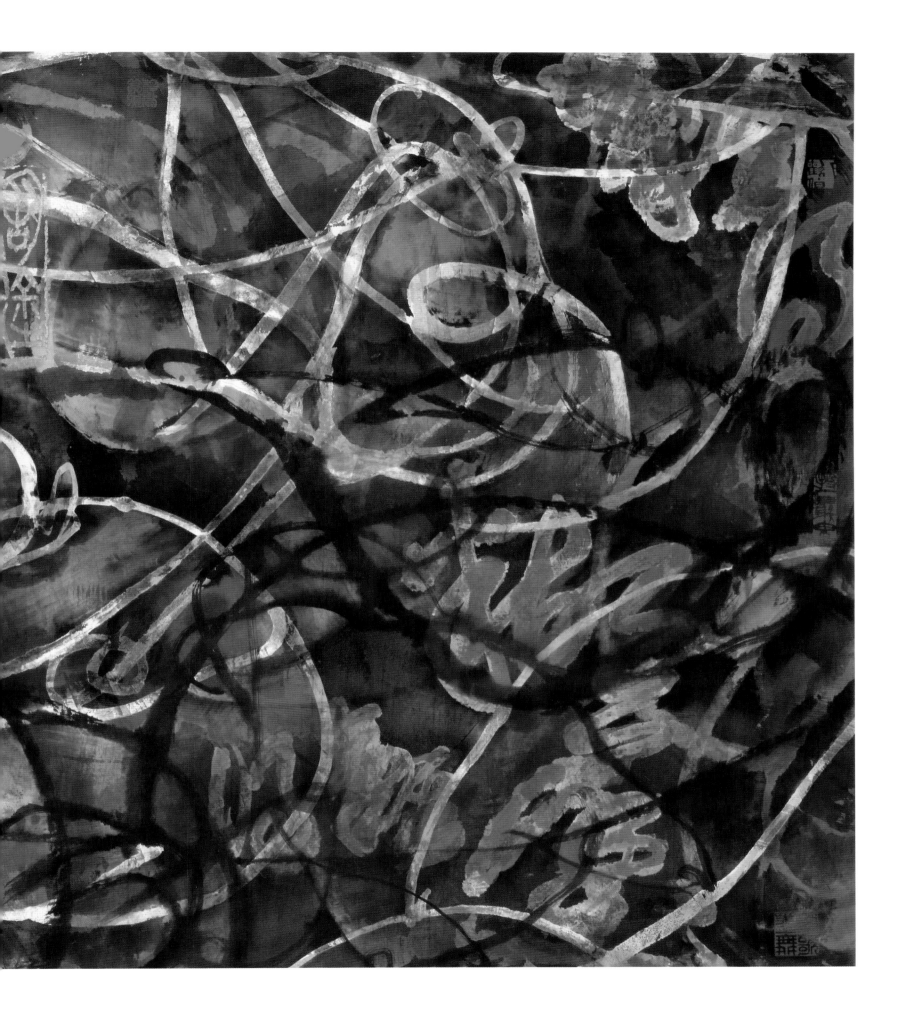

無用大用　273×170 cm　2019
Self-affirmative

無用之用是為大用。

廢紙三千何足論，翻身至理曉猶遲。狂顛究竟流行物，夢入老夫不悔時。

拈句為後現代戲法一粲耳。己亥夏日，潛龍居林章湖。

〈君子不器〉〈潛龍居〉〈林章湖〉

關渡行舟　137×68 cm　2018　畫家自藏
Legend of Guan-Du

關渡行舟，吾生得幸焉，撫此圖且拈瓦當吉語以
記之，潛龍居士林章湖，戊戌立秋后三日並題。
〈湖師〉〈壺 HUGO〉〈潛龍居〉〈掃心齋〉〈羊〉
〈洗耳〉〈十年格物〉〈迷花〉〈白頭赤子〉
〈如少水魚〉〈玉山絕頂〉〈車馬喧室〉
〈無住生心齋〉〈一粟〉
瓦當：〈長樂未央〉〈雙魚浮雲流水〉〈子孫永保〉

林章湖書畫集粹 1993 私人收藏
Album of Lin Chang-Hu Works

飄然下筆見天真。章湖學棣藉諧音作書畫，諷刺社會病態
富高妙奇趣之想像力。時甲戌新春，玉山題於容膝草堂。
〈林〉〈玉山〉

三秋　書法 8.5×34.5 cm　水墨 17×34.5 cm

三秋（篆）。童年鄉居，田庄水溝以箕撈魚比比皆是，今者良田易
工廠，水溝已污染，水清見魚之景，只能夢中想，恍然三秋。
〈生長於斯〉
三鰍（篆）。癸酉之夏，章湖。〈林印〉〈章湖〉

食祿　書法 8.5×34.5 cm　水墨 17×34.5 cm

食祿（篆）。鳥止為食亡，人則一食千金，工計盜奸而鮮仁矣。未知
樽節，過猶不及，終非本命，宜善養吾身，用世伸藏。〈清源山客〉
十鷺（篆）。癸酉之夏，章湖寫老友身影。〈林印〉〈章湖〉

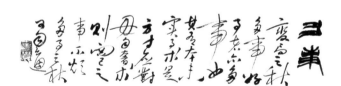

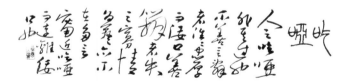

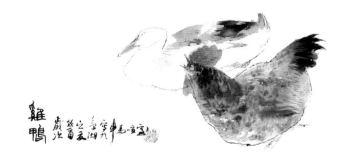

多事　書法 8.5×34.5 cm　水墨 17×34.5 cm

多事（篆）。變局之秋多事，好事者亦多事也。其有本末，實事求是，
方寸應對，毋自奢求，則關己之事不煩，多事之秋可自適。
〈十年一覽〉
多柿（篆）。歲在癸酉夏日，章湖擬之。〈林章湖〉

吃啞　書法 8.5×34.5 cm　水墨 17×34.5 cm

吃啞（篆）。人之吃啞非其過也，不善言詞者往往忠厚，而佞口善辯
者失之寡情。為藝亦不在多言，甯近吃啞而遠離佞口也。〈真意忘言〉
雞鴨（篆）。歲次癸酉之夏，章湖寫於車馬喧室。〈林章湖〉

糊塗 書法 8.5×34.5 cm 水墨 17×34.5 cm

糊塗（篆）。聰明難糊塗難，由聰明轉入糊更難，放一著退一步，
當下心安，非圖後福也。大智若愚，真難得糊塗。〈赤子心〉
壺圖（篆）。歲次癸酉梅月，章湖。〈林章湖〉

和尚 書法 8.5×34.5 cm 水墨 17×34.5 cm

和尚（篆）。心和為尚，天地自寬，無暴貪嗔之故，是能使社會祥和。
居士自持，亦可為和尚真義之別解矣。〈在家出家〉
和尚木魚青鐙，名利榮辱皆空。癸酉梅雨，登山歸來，感悟擬之，
章湖並記於車馬喧室。〈林印〉〈章湖〉

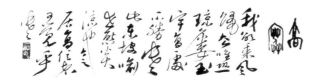

高寒 書法 8.5×34.5 cm 水墨 17×34.5 cm

高寒（篆）。我欲乘風歸去，唯恐瓊樓玉宇，高處不勝寒。此東坡
喻世態炎涼也。今之居高者可覺乎寒？〈浮雲〉
癸酉夏，章湖。〈林章湖〉

陶醉 書法 8.5×34.5 cm 水墨 17×34.5 cm

陶醉（篆）。自古正邪消長乃治亂分野。國富天下聞，而亂象滋生，
公理正義尤為長治之本。小鬼掏耳，鍾馗已醉以喻之。〈食氣〉
小鬼掏耳，鍾馗醉臥（篆）。歲在癸酉之夏，章湖自擬寫之。
〈林〉〈章湖〉

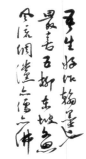

五柳 書法 20.5×15.8 cm 水墨 26×22.5 cm

吾生好作翰墨也，最喜五柳東坡，文思風流倜儻，亦儒亦佛。〈翠竹濾身〉
東籬之菊，南山之見，非菊也，非山也，得識於心是謂本相矣。章湖。〈林印〉〈章湖〉

東坡 書法 20.5×15.8 cm 水墨 26×22.5 cm

一言堂者去藝遠矣。矢志為藝須致一己之性靈，自成格局，經以權用，法必化之，乃得其真義也。〈在山泉清〉
莫聽穿林打葉聲，何妨吟嘯且徐行，竹杖芒靴輕勝馬，誰怕一簑煙雨任平生。東坡詞頗自況也。章湖。〈林章湖〉

杜甫 書法 20.5×15.8 cm 水墨 26×22.5 cm

杜工部窮而後工，可奉為右銘。在山泉水清，出山泉水濁，亂世君子，嘗自謂清流矣。
〈窮後工〉
李白 ：飯顆山頭逢杜甫，頭戴笠子日卓五，借問因何太瘦生，只為從來作詩苦。真正藝術無廉價也。章湖。〈林印〉〈章湖〉

樑楷 書法 20.5×15.8 cm 水墨 26×22.5 cm

傅山草書銳不可當，宛若飛龍在天，讀之習之復觀之，猶覺以管窺天，未及其一二也。
〈忘機〉
捨得金帶即跳脫皇帝教條也。梁瘋子真不瘋，自見蹊徑非賣弄。章湖。〈林章湖〉

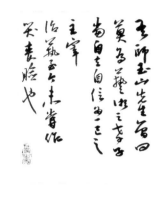

弘一　書法 20.5×15.8 cm　水墨 26×22.5 cm

若見諸相非相，即見如來，見非知是也。故凡流行之物全不可恃，須知破立之道，而致其實相矣。〈應無所住而生其心齋〉

一切有為法，如夢幻泡影，如露亦如電，應作如是觀。壬申夏遊杭州虎跑泉，訪弘一大師紀念館，瞻仰良久。精通音律美術文學而頓入空門，是孰可執孰不可執耶？人生朝露精神不死也。撫此遑恐，未覺汗手矣，章湖拜。〈林印〉〈章湖〉

喇嘛　書法 20.5×15.8 cm　水墨 26×22.5 cm

吾師玉山先生曾曰：莫為藝術之孝子，當自立自信為一己之主宰。治藝至今，未嘗作哭喪臉也。〈在家出家〉

谿聲便是廣長舌，山色豈非清淨身，夜來八萬四千偈，他日如何舉似人。東坡禪詩。章湖。〈林印〉〈章湖〉

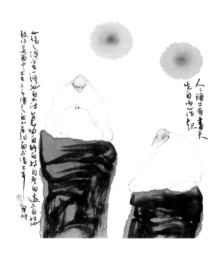

白石　書法 20.5×15.8 cm　水墨 26×22.5 cm

白石草蟲不見其小，四王山水未見其大，藝之妙處盡在一己會心玩味，故無不是之體裁。〈赤子心〉

想像白石也。章湖。見畫人像往往好似相片為稿，但乏想像之生氣也。使筆下再造栩栩如生坿之生命也。又記感言於無住生心齋。〈林章湖〉

青天　書法 20.5×15.8 cm　水墨 26×22.5 cm

谿花與禪意，相對欲忘言。余喜禪詩境遠，拈之入藝，頗況自性之得也。〈迷花〉

人人頭上有青天，先自內心作起。心境之得全在一悟也，自不待外力之功，自修自持，自參自透亦自性也。故得道箇中不在立言傳之，自心本相自求諸己耳。章湖。〈林章湖〉

千年 · 一燈　136×23 cm×2　2001　畫家自藏
A Couplet

辛巳之春，章湖。〈沉醉〉〈大象無形〉〈應無所住而生其心齋〉〈林章湖〉

陋室銘　132×70 cm　2015　畫家自藏
Inscription of Shabby Hut

陋室銘（篆）。（銘文從略）。乙未炎夏‧林章湖。
印：〈羊〉〈忘我〉〈千錯萬錯〉〈投石射鬼〉〈一片冰心〉〈應無所住而生其心齋〉〈林章湖〉〈掃心齋〉

謙卑之最 87×112 cm 2013 畫家自藏
The Most Humble

謙卑之最　玉山圓柏（篆）。臺灣玉山圓柏海拔三千五百公尺為最高灌木，其接近巔峰，姿態越低，乃是大自然謙卑之最寫照也。

（重複一遍）吾曾攻頂玉山亦感動至深也。癸巳炎夏，章湖。

〈顛倒夢想〉〈滄海一粟〉〈魔斬〉〈羊〉（3）〈一片冰心〉〈雙鵲京喜〉〈林章湖雙魚〉〈掃心齋〉

山鬼　240×69 cm　2014　畫家自藏
The Spirit of Mountain

山鬼（篆）。（文章從略）。
二〇壹四年，兩岸漢字藝術節書法以楚辭為題，吾書山鬼一首應之。
蓋其樂歌淒美感人至深，傳誦千古也。甲午炎夏六月下旬，掃心齋林章湖。
〈甲午〉〈魔斬〉〈豬行路〉〈顛倒夢想〉〈林章湖雙魚〉
〈象〉〈一片冰心〉〈素心晨夕〉〈常想一二〉〈千錯萬錯〉〈白髮三千丈〉〈忘我〉
〈掃心齋〉〈林章湖〉

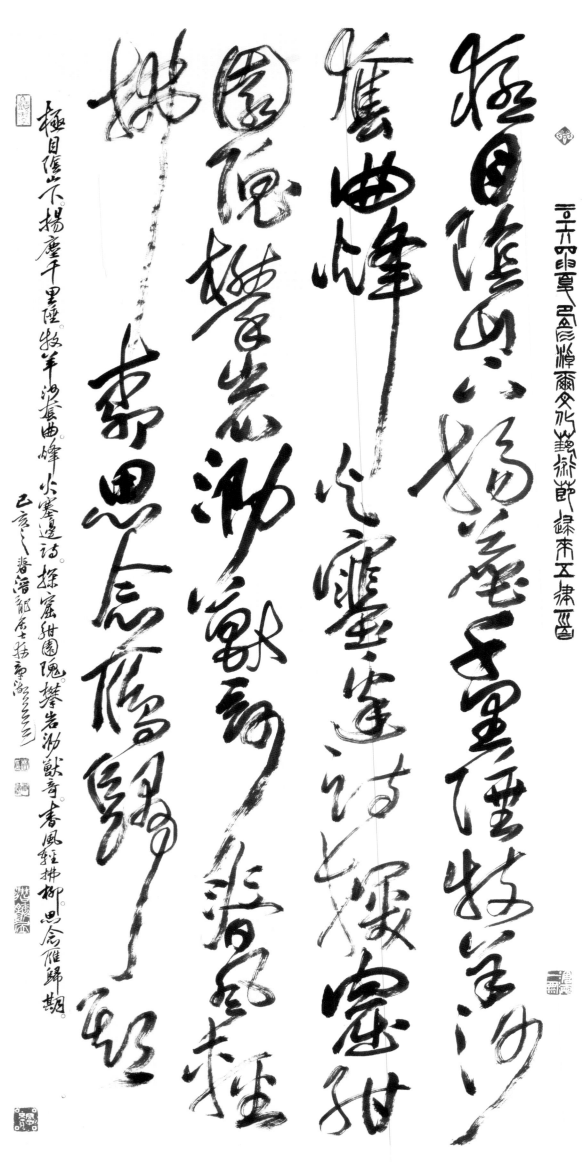

河套五律　139×70 cm　2019
Rhythm Poetry　畫家自藏

極目陰山下，揚塵千里陸。
牧羊河套曲，烽火塞邊詩。
探窟紺園隗，攀岩泖獻奇。
春風輕拂柳，思念雁歸期。
二〇一六丙申夏巴彥淖爾河套文化藝術節
歸來五律一首。

己亥之春‧潛龍居士林章湖。

〈羊〉〈滄海一粟〉〈白頭赤子〉〈林印〉
〈章湖〉〈潛龍居〉〈君子不器〉

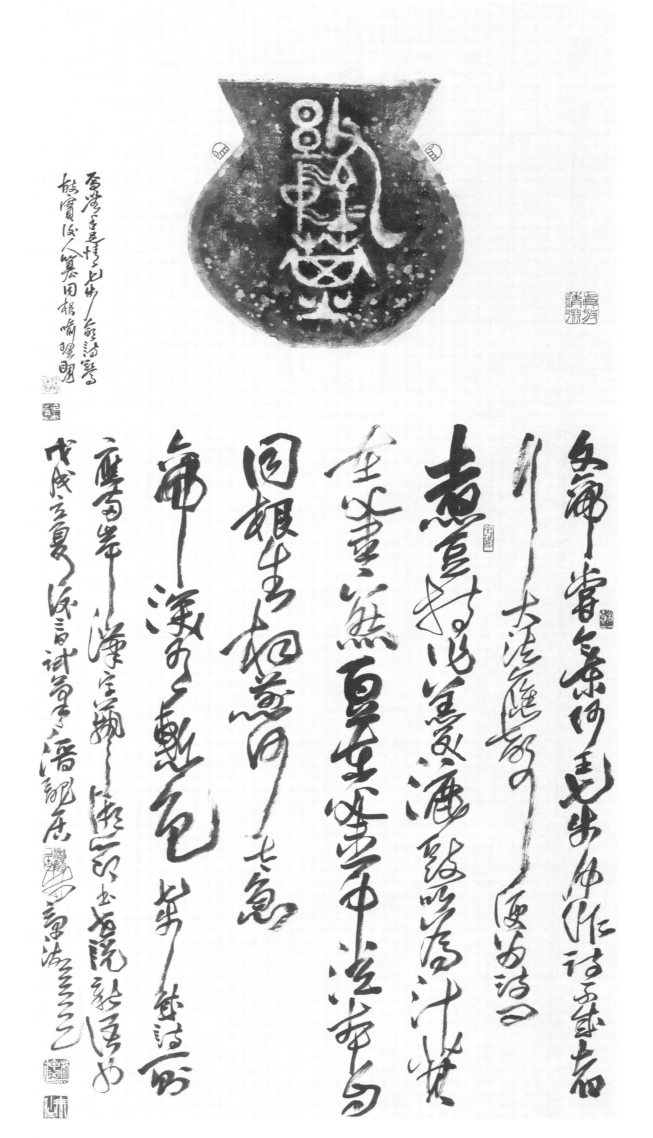

七步成詩　137×68 cm　2018
Seven Steps into a Poetry　畫家自藏

豆釜中泣其然（擬釜形銘文拓片）。
焉無手足情，七步命詩驚。
故實後人篡，同根喻理明。〈湖蟠〉
文帝嘗令東阿王七步中作詩，不成者行大法。應聲便為詩曰：「煮豆持作羹，漉豉以為汁。萁在釜下然，豆在釜中泣；本自同根生，相煎何太急？」帝深有慚色。
七步成詩一則，應兩岸漢字藝術節書世說新語也。
戊戌立夏後三日試筆，潛龍居林章湖。
〈真放精微〉〈象〉〈冷暖自知〉
〈常想一二〉〈忘機〉〈潛龍居〉
〈林章湖雙魚〉〈無住〉

131

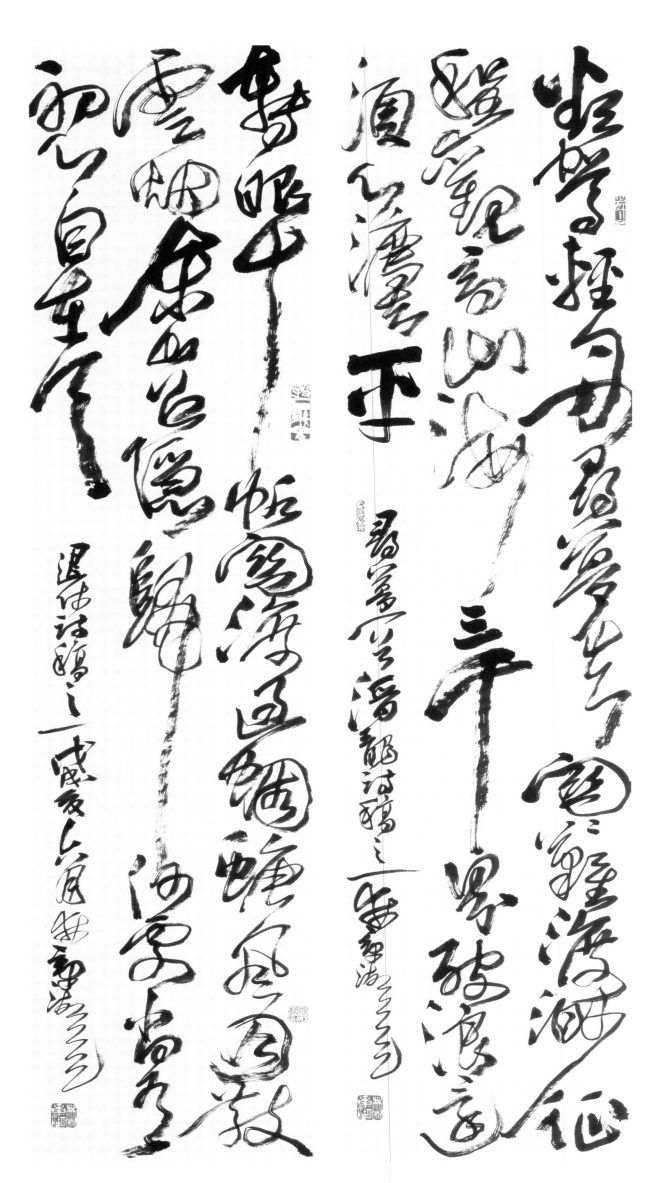

關渡詩二韻 137×34 cm×2
2018 畫家自藏
Tow Poetries of Guan-Du

欲駕輕舟尋夢去，關關難渡沙征程。
觀音山海三千界，破浪還須心法平。
尋夢一首，潛龍居詩稿之一，林章湖。
〈少年白〉〈千錯萬錯〉〈林章湖〉
轉眼千帆關渡過，蜩螗風月散雲煙。
東山招隱歸何處，尚有初心自在天。
退休詩稿之一，戊戌夏六月，林章湖。
〈投石射鬼〉〈歲月靜好〉〈林章湖〉

132

文化花瓶　136×104 cm　2019　畫家自藏
Culture Vase

花花花文化。著寫花瓶新筆法，莫論文化老生談。己亥秋，章湖。
〈千錯萬錯〉〈冷暖自知〉〈林章湖〉〈潛龍居〉

文化花瓶（篆），己亥立秋后二日利奇馬颱風方過，潛龍居，林章湖。
〈魔斬〉〈羊〉〈豬行路〉〈壺 HUGO〉〈林章湖印〉〈十年格物〉

後現代 214×139 cm 2017 桃園市立美術館橫山書法藝術館
Postmodern

後現代。今日臺灣後現代之種種，政客當道，食安問題，電話詐騙，乃至小確幸蔚為時髦等等，無不顛覆社會一般價值，可謂五花八門，魚目混珠也。

雖然後現代乃是當代之必然，但它並非藝術之萬靈丹，它之載舟覆舟實與任何主義亦無二致，端視一己思辨體用之妙耳，難以概全。吾研究後現代亦感遑遑未逮焉，揮汗並題。二〇一七年炎夏六月二十九日，潛龍居林章湖。

〈魔斬〉〈豬行路〉〈雙鵲京喜〉〈雞大吉〉〈燭淚到天明〉〈章湖雙魚〉〈無住〉〈鳳兮之歌〉〈酒歡伯〉〈燭淚到天明〉〈後來居上〉〈現在不再〉〈取而代之〉〈嘵飽剩鬧〉〈一念三千〉〈白髮三千丈〉〈羊〉〈投石射鬼〉〈一粟〉〈掃心齋〉〈白髮赤子〉〈林章湖〉。

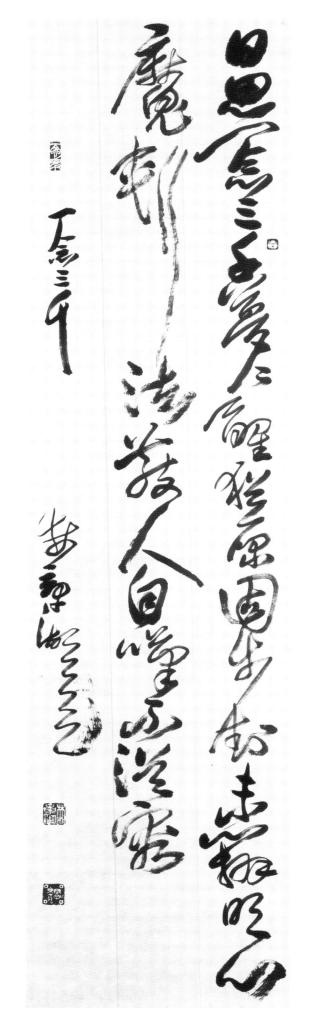

自詩　籠中鳥　137×35 cm　2019　畫家自藏
Lin Chang-Hu's Poetry

自詩　一念三千　137×35 cm　2019　畫家自藏
Lin Chang-Hu's Poetry

東山無遠志，破屋畏西風。老驥垂槽櫪，幽蛟隱碧空。
盤桓潮浪沒，鬱結俗網終。一落籠中鳥，何由勝本衷。
籠中鳥。林章湖。〈浮雲〉〈歲月靜好〉〈林章湖〉

日思一念三千夢，夢醒猶原因步封。
未辨明心魔斬法，凡夫自嘆不從容。
一念三千。林章湖。〈豬〉〈一念三千〉〈林章湖〉〈君子不器〉

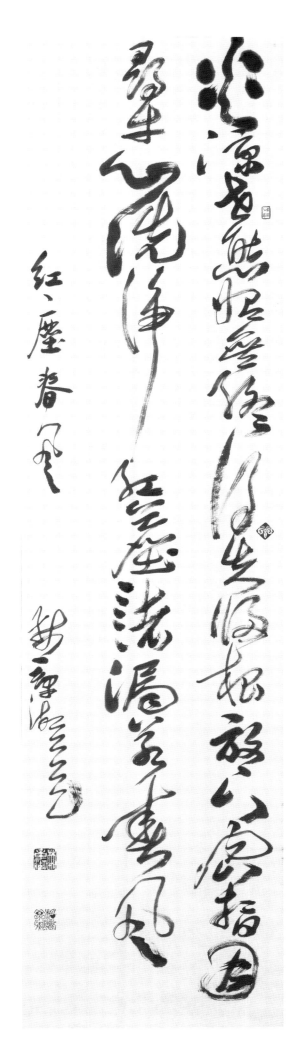

自詩 紅塵春風 137×35 cm 2019 畫家自藏
Lin Chang-Hu's Poetry

炎涼世態始無終，得失歸根放下空。
指月尋牛心洗淨，紅塵諸漏若春風。
紅塵春風。林章湖。〈瑤林仙館〉〈羊〉〈林章湖〉〈顛倒夢想〉

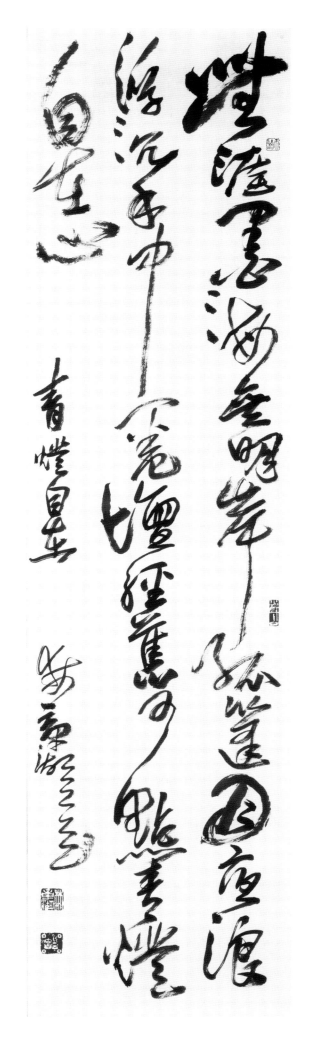

自詩 青燈自在 137×35 cm 2019 畫家自藏
Lin Chang-Hu's Poetry

無涯墨海無明岸，孤篷月夜浪浮沉。
手中一卷壇經舊，可點青燈自在心。
青燈自在。林章湖。〈天聽〉〈少年白〉〈林章湖〉〈君子不器〉

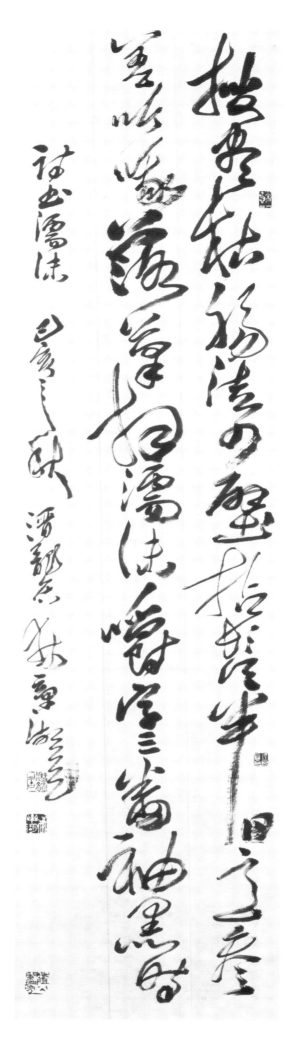

自詩 趙偉師贈墨　137×35 cm　2019　畫家自藏
Lin Chang-Hu's Poetry

自詩 詩書濡沫　137×35 cm　2019　畫家自藏
Lin Chang-Hu's Poetry

尚憶京華一夢鄉，還磨古墨泛滄桑。清風在耳應猶記，落筆詩書歲月長。
趙偉師贈墨研之一揮，潛龍居林章湖。
〈浮雲〉〈穿石〉〈林章湖印〉〈在山泉清〉〈冷耳聽語〉

搜盡枯腸徒四壁，拈鬚半日意參差。吟哦落筆相濡沫，嚼字三番袖黑時。
詩書濡沫。己亥之秋，潛龍居林章湖。
〈常想一二〉〈迷花〉〈潛龍居〉〈林章湖〉〈燈火闌珊處〉（阮常耀刻）

自詩 雷雨驚夢 137×35 cm 2019 畫家自藏
Lin Chang-Hu's Poetry

雨聲雷鼓到三更，落枕無言畫裡驚。紙破墨翻天盡黑，荁來道濟笑經營。
雷雨驚夢。己亥之秋，林章湖。
〈鬼迷心竅〉〈林章湖印〉〈在山泉清〉〈忘塵〉

自詩 海印三昧 137×35 cm 2019 畫家自藏
Lin Chang-Hu's Poetry

三昧還聽法鼓鐘，圓通諸漏伏龍蹤。印空一悟風吹盡，自性了然四海同。
海印三昧（篆）。法鼓山題字刻石。吾詩忝題之。己亥之秋，潛龍居章湖。
〈穿石〉〈顛倒夢想〉〈歲月靜好〉〈一念三千〉〈林〉〈章湖〉〈苦集滅道〉

139

題〈煙雨瘦西湖〉〈象〉

遊湖三月濛濛雨,黛柳煙花暗塢飛,騷酒微醺人豈醉,揚州一別夢依依。

題〈富春翠微〉〈車馬喧室〉

蓬舟依渡口,遇雨暮雲迴。幾夜花開落,櫓搖夢底催。

題〈太行卦壁〉〈常想一二〉

不肯藏山墅,年年苦鑿雕。愚公拼血汗,壁道貫迢迢。

窗外山茶二韻(一〇八研究室窗外)〈無悔〉

春雨催花豔,朝陽蕊滴珠。倚窗低嘆賞,寫意入心湖。
研墨每興歎,推敲鬢已寒。山空人惜老,暮想筆闌珊。

題〈玉峰映霞〉〈浮雲〉

排雲咫尺望尖峰,肉腳攀登尚滌胸。向晚秋霞天幻影,何尋俠侶射鵰蹤。

題〈玉頂彤雲〉〈窮後工〉

強攻玉頂稱豪氣,自負雲山望海遙。消長迷藏歸本性,浮鳶冷嘯寄九霄。

鰲鼓濕地寫生二首〈日日新〉

諸羅鰲鼓沼泥地,夕照群鷗錯落微,埃及聖禽新報到,嘉南自此更奇稀。
初晨映日波光晃,蕩游群禽覓食忙,速寫匆匆風颯颯,獨棲傑克近身旁。
(傑克乃一折翼鸕鶿之別名,不得北返,已成留鳥也)

題〈留住傘洲〉〈大吉大利〉

潮神日夜侵沙島,暗使波臣噬竹寮,勢破蚵棚漂散岸,徒留鷗鷺最逍遙。

林辛湖印集

北岳

壺 HUGO

大象無形

道法自然

掃心齋

有鳳初鳴

玉山絕頂

一念三千

常想一二

晴窗。

〈無往不復〉〈歐介〉〈豪年長壽〉

登土城天上山〈素心晨夕〉

可比黃山景，登臨不勝收。天山屏眾壑，大漢攏支流。
挹翠鳶翔嘯，危龕壁彩脩。沉鐘催暮色，且記岸回頭。

題〈日月桐脩〉（土城創辦桐花節至今已二十二年矣）〈在家出家〉

清源日月禪房寂，落雪桐花法雨飄。念佛餐風僧渡眾，蓬萊小乘盛
今朝。

題〈澤平皓月〉〈放下〉

凤汐鳧鷗集，澤平皓月低，幽人應未寐，世局亂潮淒。

題〈江河晚歌〉〈赤子心〉

觀春潮暗雨，渡瑟瑟江河。下筆心驚恐，低迴唱晚歌。

詠土城承天寺〈車馬喧室〉

小乘傳臺海，廣公筆故庭；獼猴朝獻果，猛虎夕聞經。
日月清源照，天山熱谷冥；桐花開若雪，信眾上高亭。

廣欽上人弘法〈車馬喧室〉

渡海欽公法，泉州伏虎僧。羸身茹素果，孤影伴青燈。
普雨無明業，承天有梵龍。無來無去偈，勸世了貪矜。

謁廣欽上人法堂〈冷暖自知〉

煙嵐淡海染紅塵，渺渺觀音影事泯。
一謁廣公堂上相，蓮開並蒂洗凡身。

潛龍居詩稿　2018　36×675 cm
A Scroll of the Manuscript of Po

湖海嘯吟
韓潮蘇海文瀾壯，林子章湖藝意奇。
我再新詩為題卷，毫端墨彩态紛披。
昔吟今又易句成此，章湖道盟一粲。
庚子元日，八十六歲歐毫年，天寬樓
〈白首名山自頡頏〉〈天風伴嘯吟〉

寄莊明中博士〈冷暖自知〉
喜鵲知音相伴讀，莊生抱負勝隆冬。博班滿志明中月，怎憶寒窗
有幾重。

馬尾祭三首（五言絕句）〈羊〉
白髮雖言老，偏留馬尾鬃。靈犀來搞怪，現代論無雙。
壯志焉愁失，躊躇四海遊。年資應早了，退隱怨言休。
六法嘗何盡，功名亦屬空。人生興廢事，至此笑談中。

鐘鼓樓觀想　〈瑤林仙館〉
問君營利火，樓鼓渺無踪，一任權謀鑿，何關世道從。
孤僧圓匯款，大願憫聞鐘，若作雙樓喻，遑言俗聖共。

關渡回首〈羊〉
朝夕虹橋過，觀音倒影寒，紅林樓候鳥，漲水浸漁竿。
夜冷孤鴻咽，譏多處士難，無情潮汐弄，忍教一身單。

題〈秋泉雲僧〉〈天聽〉
莫問空樓鼓，猶聞洗耳鐘；交鋒分異己，相諍辨真宗。
幾度崇洋調，三番數典蹤；雲心與鶴眼，退士寓於胸。

退隱自遣　〈迷花〉
匆匆卅載浮生夢，得失如煙醒亦矇，關渡何曾觀自在，白頭豈教悟虛空。
明知博士殘雲過，慣看官銜化糞同，俯仰心齋無罣礙，悠哉日日墨池中。

雞大吉

魚躍龍門

豬行路

真放精微

雙鵲京喜

北海十年

在山泉清

酒歡伯

鳳兮之歌

魔斬

噍飽剩閧

投石射鬼

白頭赤子

苦集滅道

歲月靜好

聖嚴法師偈

潛龍居

五風十雨

143

如少水魚

之趣矢洎之乱乃现焉
稚末能惇之坐石樓揁
爲音㖗雁偃㗢伯契合
以配兰方吵吵三字也
魚刻白文鶳形極简

刻之是爲白揚之
吾吿已满半盤
晋贤六書兰薩偶之二可
吾合誰揁之
相为㖗雁自出己臆
越貊断龀之
試以鳥形午字横思

章漱玉
王音泛

君子不器

乱子窗卿
尾此印石
色泽圭黄
新有花纹
坐顶地钤
之寿山硬黄
强为心力
作斑玟状
红色金石
圭之二斗
此石靖於
山东曲阜
孔林衔坊
艺呂君中
吾是送此花
往细玫旦
尺寸猾六哑
刻於孔子名言
用佛心画此

144

飛相掃心

應無所住而生其心齋

燭淚到天明

無住

十年格物

冷暖自知

水窮雲起

洗耳

林章湖 大事記年表

1955 ・出生於臺灣臺北縣土城大安寮外祖農家，七歲就讀土城國小

1963 ・九歲隨父親林士英公職調臺北縣澳底漁港，轉學澳底國小三年級，始承庭訓，臨帖習畫奠定傳統基礎

1967 ・臺北縣雙溪初中時期，承韓玉梁、周清助老師指導，校內外學生美術、書法與漫畫比賽名列前茅

1970 ・宜蘭高中時期，承齊白石弟子田縝之老師、魏得璇老師指導，宜蘭縣學生競賽國畫第二名、書法第一名

1973 ・國立臺灣師範大學美術系時期，受業於林玉山、呂佛庭、張德文、陳銀輝、王秀雄、梁秀中、羅芳、傅佑武、王壯為、王北岳等教授

1977 ・國立臺灣師範大學美術系展國畫第一名、篆刻第二名
・國立臺灣師範大學美術系畢業展國畫第一名、書法第二名
・第五屆國家文藝獎（大專美術獎）

1979 ・國立國父紀念館典藏水墨〈中和勝地〉

1982 ・由積穗國中美術老師轉任國立藝術學院美術系助教
・就讀國立臺灣師範大學美術研究所，受業於黃君璧、林玉山、鄭善禧、李霖燦、劉文潭等教授

1983 ・教育部文藝創作獎國畫第二名
・國立臺灣藝術教育館典藏水墨〈古廟〉
・受邀「國際水墨聯展」，韓國漢城

1985 ・教育部遴選為「世界青年藝術節」代表，赴美國華盛頓、牙買加金斯頓書畫表演

1986 ・國立臺灣師範大學美術研究所碩士，李霖燦教授指導碩士論文《元代王蒙山水畫風格之研究》，國科會獎助論文
・升等國立藝術學院美術系專任講師
・受邀「中日美術交換展」，日本東京
・受邀「中國傳統繪畫之新潮流聯展」，法國凡爾賽市

1987 ・教育部文藝創作獎國畫第一名
・國立臺灣藝術教育館典藏水墨〈月世界〉
・受邀「中華民國美術發展」展覽，臺灣省立美術館

1988 ・林章湖畫展，臺北市立美術館，出版畫冊《林章湖畫選》
・臺北市立美術館典藏水墨〈小谿之晨〉〈芒野白鷺〉〈月夜〉〈蒼鷹〉
・受邀「中韓水墨交流展」，臺北，漢城
・當代書畫美國五年巡迴展，參展水墨作品〈春寒〉，國立歷史博物館

1989 ・第一屆大陸吳作人國際青年美術獎，中國美協主席吳作人題贈書法〈華香兩岸〉
・擔任臺灣省第44屆全省美展國畫評審委員
・赴美藝文訪問團，太平洋文化基金會

1990 ・大地徜徉：林章湖創作展，臺灣省立美術館，出版畫冊《大地徜徉：林章湖畫展》
・臺北縣立文化中心典藏水墨〈冬濤〉

1991 ・林昌德、程代勒、林章湖三人絲路行，遊歷華山、敦煌、火州、烏魯木齊等地，創作《巴札市集》人物畫手卷
・林章湖畫展，臺北縣立文化中心，出版畫冊《林章湖畫展》
・臺灣省立美術館典藏水墨〈夜饗圖〉
・擔任臺灣省第46屆全省美展國畫評審委員

1992 ・出版著作《關河夢：林章湖藝術心路》，京華藝術中心
・升等國立藝術學院美術系專任副教授
・擔任臺灣省第47屆全省美展國畫評審委員

1993 ・擔任臺灣省立美術館展品審查委員

1995 ・飛相掃心：林章湖書畫展，臺灣省立美術館，出版畫冊《飛相掃心：林章湖書畫展》

師大水墨教學重視寫生為基礎，林章湖以筆墨實地練習

1977 林章湖獲師大美術系展國畫第一名，與63級學長林玉山（右）合影

1983 林章湖（左三）就讀師大美術研究所，於黃君璧教授（左一）白雲堂上課，呂燕卿（右一）、林達隆（左二）

1985 世界青年藝術節，林章湖路經美國華盛頓DC，特地向佛利爾東方美術館館長傅申博士請益碩士論文

1989 林章湖獲第一屆大陸吳作人國際青年美術獎，吳作人先生夫人（中），林章湖（左五）

1990 大地徜徉：林章湖創作展，臺灣省立美術館，全家合影。

1995 林章湖飛相掃心書畫展，恩師林玉山教授賜序文，於容膝草堂拜觀其《黃山寫生》冊頁

1996 當代著名研究收藏八大山人學者王方宇（中）參觀林章湖書畫展，右為羲之堂總經理陳筱君

1996 ・臺灣省立美術館典藏水墨〈清流圖卷〉
　　 ・發表專文「白石老人畫蝦風格初探」，《白石畫冊》，國立歷史
　　　 博物館

1997 ・出版著作《自在理想主義》，義之堂
　　 ・升等國立藝術學院美術系專任教授
　　 ・文建會全國文藝季「土城朝山桐花節」，擔任藝術指導
　　 ・愛爾蘭藝術設計學院客座教授，都柏林
　　 ・高雄市立美術館典藏水墨〈諸法無相〉

1999 ・首屆傳統與實驗書藝雙年展應邀參展，何創時書藝基金會
　　 ・輔仁大學應用美術系兼任教授，承林文昌系主任延聘

2000 ・林章湖書畫：愛爾蘭東方博物館開館首展，並典藏書法及水墨
　　　 〈九雞圖〉
　　 ・愛爾蘭奧斯特大學藝術中心書畫示範，貝爾法斯特市
　　 ・國立臺灣藝術學院美術系兼任教授，承羅振賢系主任延聘

2001 ・國立臺北藝術大學美術系所主任、美術史研究所長
　　 ・「現代書法新展望」兩岸學術交流研討會，擔任特約討論人，
　　　 國立臺灣美術館

2002 ・國立臺北藝術大學美術學院院長、美術史研究所長
　｜ ・關渡花卉藝術節，擔任藝術總監，國立臺北藝術大學與行政院
2007　 農委會共同舉辦三屆活動

2002 ・擔任何創時書藝基金會顧問
　　 ・齊白石大展研討會，國立國父紀念館中山講堂，義之堂、中國
　　　 時報系
　　 ・嶽鎮川靈—江兆申書畫藝術國際學術研討會，擔任主持人，國
　　　 立臺北藝術大學

2003 ・忘塵：林章湖畫展，義之堂，出版畫冊《忘塵：林章湖畫集》
　　 ・受邀「臺灣水墨畫家聯展」，河南博物館
　　 ・受邀「華夏名人名家書畫作品聯展」，臺北、北京

2004 ・中華民國畫學會金爵獎
　　 ・隨鄭善禧教授赴西藏旅遊寫生，歸來創作西藏系列作品

2005 ・傳統與實驗書藝雙年展，發表專文「心畫殊勝，斬魔揮灑」，
　　　 何創時書藝基金會
　　 ・受邀「漢字書藝大展」，中正紀念堂中正藝廊
　　 ・台灣當代水墨名家大展，北京文化部交流中心，觀想藝術公司
　　 ・台灣當代名家美術展，沙烏地阿拉伯國立博物館
　　 ・擔任全國美術展覽會國畫評審委員
　　 ・受邀「海峽兩岸書畫藝術聯展」，福建省美術館
　　 ・獲邀編入〈台灣現代美術大系〉水墨畫家，行政院文建會

2006 ・三明治時光：林章湖書畫展，台灣創價學會，出版畫冊《三明
　　　 治時光：林章湖書畫集》，典藏書畫〈漁村舊事〉〈野銀部落〉
　　　 〈觀魚〉等十二件作品
　　 ・水墨三劍客聯展：李蕭錕、林章湖、程代勒，福華沙龍
　　 ・新加坡書法中心聯展，光前堂
　　 ・擔任第十屆國家文藝獎評審委員
　　 ・「當代書畫藝術發展回顧與展望」國際學術研討會，擔任主
　　　 持人與特約討論人，國立臺灣藝術大學
　　 ・受邀「台北、杭州書法展」，杭州西湖美術館

2007 ・三明治時光：林章湖書畫展，宜蘭縣立文化中心
　　 ・翰墨千秋：台灣當代書法風貌大展，中正紀念堂
　　 ・高雄市立美館典藏水墨〈金灣濤聲〉
　　 ・國立臺灣美術館典藏水墨〈一夜鄉心〉
　　 ・受邀胡志明市台灣學校中華藝文活動，教學示範

1997 林章湖擔任全國文藝季土城朝山
桐花節藝術指導，並為民眾導覽

2000 林章湖於愛爾蘭東方博物館開館
首展開幕致詞，我駐愛爾蘭代表李明亮
（左一）、愛爾蘭東方博物館館長（左二）

2000 林章湖受邀愛爾蘭奧斯特大學藝
術中心，為該校藝術系師生現場書畫
示範介紹

2002 齊白石大展：左起臺灣大學藝史
所教授傅申、臺北藝大美術學院院長
林章湖、榮寶齋藝術總監雷振芳、師
大美研所所長袁金塔、故宮書畫處處
長王耀庭、著名藝評家郎紹君、故宮
博物院副院長石守謙

2004 西藏旅遊寫生，林章湖與鄭善禧
教授同遊，歸來創作西藏系列作品

2004 西藏旅遊寫生，於薩迦寺喇嘛辯
經休息時速寫補捉其造型神態

2006 台北杭州書法展開幕，於浙江西
湖美術館，左起黃智陽、王冬齡、黃
一鳴、林章湖、蔡明讚

臺北藝大美術系水墨傳統技法課程，
林章湖講解並示範宋人工筆花鳥畫法

2008 ・雲遊：林章湖書畫展，土城藝文館，出版畫冊《雲遊：2008 林章湖書畫集》
・中國文化大學藝術研究所兼任教授，承歐豪年教授延聘
・擔任第四十三屆中山文藝獎評審委員
・受邀「台日文化交流書藝大展」，國立臺灣民主紀念館
・受邀「兩岸三地當代書畫名家聯展」，舊金山灣區

2009 ・受邀世界書藝全北雙年展，參展書法〈醉翁之意在山水間〉，韓國全羅北道
・受邀「兩岸新象當代水墨展」，國立臺灣美術館
・受邀創作臺灣名卉八品：〈鐵線蓮〉，國立歷史博物館
・受邀「中國山水畫學術邀請展暨文化高峰論壇」，采風寫生，四川省文化廳

2010 ・獲頒臺北藝大屆滿 30 年資深優良教師
・國立臺北藝術大學教授退休
・赴北京中央美術學院攻讀博士
・受邀「第一屆兩岸漢字藝術節」，參展書法作品〈醉翁之意〉，北京
・臺灣美術院院士

2011 ・臺灣書畫百年大展，中山國家畫廊，國立國父紀念館
・新富春山居圖兩岸名家聯展，參展水墨作品〈富春翠微〉並承典藏，中國國家博物館
・國立臺灣師範大學美術系博碩士班兼任教授

2012 ・當代中國畫學術論壇，中山國家畫廊，國立國父紀念館
・中國文字博物館典藏書法〈烏衣巷〉，中國安陽市

2013 ・中央美術學院美術學博士（Ph. D.），博士論文：《「後現代」與臺灣當代水墨》
・兩岸水墨畫家揚州大運河寫生，江蘇省美術館展覽

2014 ・問道無心：林章湖書畫展，臺中市立大墩文化中心，出版畫冊《問道無心：林章湖書畫展》
・出版畫冊《林章湖作品集》，溢泰實業有限公司
・受邀「台灣 50 現代水墨展」，築空間
・香港蘇富比公司春季拍賣成交：水墨〈白楊莊稼〉

2015 ・山東臺灣館書畫聯展，山東濰坊
・西安臺北水墨交流展，臺灣師大德群藝廊
・北京中華文化論壇，北京大學

2016 ・韓國首爾東國大學客座教授，並遊歷慶州佛國寺、石窟庵等
・「林玉山的創作與傳承」聯展，參展水墨作品〈伏虎調心〉，中華文化復興總會
・卅年看山：林章湖書畫展，彰化生活美學館，出版畫冊《卅年看山：林章湖書畫展》
・出版博士論文《「後現代」與臺灣當代水墨》，花木蘭出版社

2017 ・全球水墨畫大展，參展水墨作品〈糊塗無極〉，香港會議展覽中心
・擔任明宗書法獎評審，高雄明宗書法館

2018 ・受邀為法鼓山刻石題字：〈海印三昧〉並賦詩七絕一首
・杭州市連橫紀念館十週年，青山青史兩岸藝術名家書畫聯展，並典藏三件作品

2019 ・第九屆兩岸漢字藝術節兩岸名家書法展，內蒙古美術館
・〈臺灣風情〉當代 12 位水墨畫家合繪大畫，國立國父紀念館
・受邀日本新構造社，「第 91 回新構造社展」，日本東京都美術館
・桃園市立美術館橫山書法藝術館，典藏書法〈後現代〉

2020 ・臺灣美術院十週年院士大展，國立國父紀念館博愛藝廊
・潛龍勿用：林章湖書畫展，國立國父紀念館中山國家畫廊，出版畫冊《2020 潛龍勿用—林章湖書畫展》

2007 臺北藝大與中央美院交流，左起林章湖、潘公凱院長、朱宗慶校長

2009 在國立歷史博物館國家畫廊與張大千嫡傳弟子孫家勤教授畫展時合影

2011 新富春山居圖兩岸名家聯展，與前中國美術館長楊力舟在參展水墨作品〈富春翠微〉前合影

2013 兩岸畫家揚州大運河寫生，江蘇省美術館展覽，與中國國家博物館呂章生前館長在展品〈煙雨瘦西湖〉前合影

2013 林章湖博士學位答辯通過，與兩位博導李少文、羅世平教授合影

2014 台灣 50 現代水墨展，台開董事長邱復生（左一）、林章湖、羲之堂總經理陳筱君（右一）

2015 春酒雅集，林章湖與歐豪年教授天寬樓畫室筆繪

2020 臺灣美術院十週年院士大展，院士成員合影，廖修平院長（前排左三）、王秀雄榮譽董事長（前排左四）、林章湖（後排左一）

Biography of Lin Chang-Hu

Dr. Lin was born in 1955, Tucheng district, New Taipei City, Taiwan.

He is Master of Fine Arts at Taiwan Normal University and Fine Arts of Ph.D. at China Central Academy of Fine Arts.

Current positions	Founded artist of Taiwan Fine Arts Academy
	Consultant of Ho's Calligraphy Foundation
Personal Experience	Visiting professor at National College of Art and Design in Dublin, Ireland
	Full-time professor, department chairman, graduate school director of History of Arts, and dean of school of Fine Arts at Taipei National University of the Arts
	Part-time professor at National Taiwan Normal University of Arts, Fu-Jen Catholic University, and Chinese Cultural University
	Judge/Consultant at City Art Exhibitions, National Art Exhibitions, National Festival of Culture and Arts, ROC National Art Exhibitions, Dr. Sun, Yat-Sen Culture and Arts Award, and National Culture and Arts Award
Solo Exhibitions	Taipei Fine Arts Museum,1988
	National Taiwan Museum of Fine Arts,1990、1995
	The Cultural Center in New Taipei City,1991
	The Chester Beatty Library Dublin, Ireland,2000
	Xi Zhi Tang Gallery,2003
	Art Centers of Taiwan Soka Association,2006
	Yilan County Cultural Affairs Bureau,2007
	Art Center of Tucheng, 2008
	The Cultural Center in Taichung City, 2014
	The Cultural Center in changhua City 2016
	National Gallery, National Sun Yat-sen Memorial Hall 2020
International Exhibitions	International Ink Painting Exhibition and Symposium, Taipei
	International Maestro Calligraphy and Painting Exhibition, Taipei
	Academic Forum of Contemporary Chinese Painting, Taipei
	Cross-Strait Maestro Chinese Painting Exhibition, Taipei
	Cross-Strait Chinese Character Arts Festival, Taipei

Thesis	A Study of Landscape Painting Style of Wang Meng in Yuan Dynasty, National Taiwan Normal University
	Preliminary Research on Qi Baishi's Shrimp Painting Style, National Museum of History
	My Ink　Painting Discussion of Ease and Idealism, Xi Zhi Tang Gallery
	Qi Baishi's Elaborate-Style Painting, Freehand Brushwork, and Lifelikeness, National Taiwan University of Arts
	The Acme of Perfection by Unrestricted Creative Writing, Ho's Calligraphy Foundation
	"Postmodern" and Taiwan Contemporary Ink Painting, China Central Academy of Fine Arts
Collections Conservation	National Dr. Sun Yat-Sen Memorial Hall
	National Taiwan Arts Education Center
	Taipei Fine Arts Museum
	National Taiwan Museum of Fine Arts
	Kaohsiung Museum of Fine Arts
	Cultural Affairs Department of New Taipei City Government
	The Chester Beatty Library Dublin, Ireland
Awards	1977 First Prize, Inkpainting, Second Prize, Sealcarving, in Department of Fine Arts Exhibition at Taiwan Normal University
	1977 National Culture and Arts Award
	1987 First Prize on Chinese Painting Category, Cultural and Art Creation Awards of Ministry of Education
	1989 Fine Arts Award of First Wu Zuo-ren International Awards, China
	2004 Golden Tripod Award, ROC Painting Association
Albums	1988 Selected Works of Lin Chang-Hu, Taipei Fine Arts Museum
	1990 Leisure of Nature, National Taiwan Museum of Fine Arts
	1991 Lin Chang-Hu Exhibition, Taipei County Cultural Center
	1995 Beyond the Appearance, National Taiwan Museum of Fine Arts
	2003 The Image of Traveler, Xi Zhi Tang Gallery
	2006 Sandwich Time, Taiwan Soka Association
	2008 Wandering, Art Center of Tucheng
	2014 Lin Chang-Hu's Calligraphy ＆ Painting，Yitai Company
	2014 Unintentionally, Taichung City Dadun Cultural Center
	2016 Drawing Mountains for 30 Years, National Chunghua Living Art Center
	2020 Hidden Dragon, Do not Act, National Gallery, Sun Yat-sen Memorial Hall

出版品左起
1988《林章湖畫選》
1997《自在理想主義》
2014《林章湖作品集》
2016《「後現代」與臺灣當代水墨》

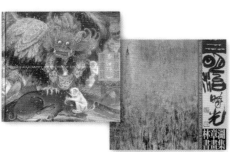

出版品左起
1995《飛相掃心：林章湖書畫展》
2006《三明治時光：林章湖書畫集》
2008《雲遊：2008 林章湖書畫集》
2014《問道無心：林章湖書畫展》
2016《卅年看山：林章湖書畫展》

2020 潛龍勿用——林章湖書畫展
2020 Hidden Dragon, Do not Act –
Lin Chang-hu Ink Painting and Calligraphy Exhibition

發　　行	梁永斐
出　　版	國立國父紀念館
	地址：11073 臺北市信義區仁愛路四段 505 號
	電話：+886-2-2758-8008
	傳真：+886-2-8780-1082
	網址：http://www.yatsen.gov.tw
封面題字	林章湖
總 編 輯	楊同慧
執行編輯	楊得聖、汪麗清
策 展 人	陳筱君
美術設計	游明龍設計有限公司
印刷製作	飛燕印刷有限公司
出版日期	2020 年 2 月
定　　價	新臺幣 2,000 元整
GPN	1010900183
ISBN	978-986-532-033-1（精裝）

展售處

國家書店【松江門市】臺北市中山區松江路 209 號 1 樓
TEL: +886-2-2518-0207 FAX: +886-2-2518-0778

五南文化廣場【臺中總店】臺中市中山路 6 號
TEL: +886-4-2226-0330 FAX: +886-4-2225-8234
網路書局：http://www.wunanbooks.com.tw/

大手事業有限公司（博愛堂）【國父紀念館門市】
TEL: +886-2-8789-4640 FAX: +886-2-2218-7929

Bigtom 美國冰淇淋咖啡館【翠湖店】
TEL: +886-2-2345-4213 FAX: +886-2-2723-8417
臺北市光復南路 306 號對面（國立國父紀念館光復南路入口處右側）
http://www.bigtom.us

國家圖書館出版品預行編目 (CIP) 資料

2020 潛龍勿用：林章湖書畫展 / 楊同慧總編輯 .-- 臺北市
：國父紀念館 , 2020.02
　　面；　公分
ISBN 978-986-532-033-1(精裝)
1. 書畫 2. 篆刻 3. 作品集

941.5　　　　　　　　　　109000482

ISBN-13: 978-986-532-033-1
02000